A Planning Framework for the Green New Deal

Planning a Sustainable Future:
How New Towns Can Transform the Economy and Save Our Only Home Before it is too Late

Duane Errol Fleming

WESTBOW
PRESS®
A DIVISION OF THOMAS NELSON
& ZONDERVAN

WestBow Press books may be ordered through booksellers or by contacting:

WestBow Press
A Division of Thomas Nelson & Zondervan
1663 Liberty Drive
Bloomington, IN 47403
www.westbowpress.com
1 (866) 928-1240

ISBN: 978-1-9736-7057-5 (sc)
ISBN: 978-1-9736-7059-9 (hc)
ISBN: 978-1-9736-7058-2 (e)

Library of Congress Control Number: 2019910642

Print information available on the last page.

WestBow Press rev. date: 08/20/2019

This book is dedicated to women and men of good will who are working "to advance the forward days of humankind," as Buckminster Fuller was fond of doing.

Contents

Introduction

A Planning Framework for the Green New Deal proposes long-range planning solutions to our most critical problems:

1. We must rapidly reduce and eliminate carbon dioxide and methane in the atmosphere by providing renewable energy and safe nuclear reactors.
2. We need to create forty-seven million sustainable jobs to replace those that will be eliminated by automation.
3. We need to build massive amounts of affordable housing for the workforce.
4. We need to replace gas-powered cars with renewable energy cars and rapid mass transit.
5. We need to replace the shareholder-dominated economic structure with worker-owned cooperatives that pay a livelihood wage and offer health care and a comfortable retirement in exchange for a lifetime of work. Capitalism needs to be reformed but not totally abandoned, but greed for more and more money cannot be its sole priority. We need to distribute wealth at the workplace, giving people a good life.

All of these projects can be accomplished by using a new town planning framework. By using this framework, we can use all the advanced knowledge of economists, city planners, architects, engineers, and farmers. We will be able to use best practices and new technologies, including recycling and regenerative agriculture and forestry to create carbon dioxide sinks and advance the forward days of humankind with an urgent and uniting work effort. There are many, many individual projects being proposed to be in the Green New Deal. What is also needed is a vision and a planning framework within new towns to develop all of our good and sustainable projects.

Liquid Fluoride Thorium Nuclear Reactors (LFTRs)

As we shall see, these safe molten salt mini-reactors will be needed to rapidly scale up electricity production from non-carbon sources, providing electricity 24/7. This will solve the battery storage problem when the wind doesn't blow and the sun doesn't shine, and it will reduce the use of natural gas.

There is hope for a modestly abundant future, but only if the nation

- shifts resources from the military-industrial complex (MIC) to a nation-building at home complex in order to provide for our real national interests,
- develops a national energy and transportation plan to stop burning fossil fuels and reduce gasoline-powered driven cars by 66 percent, by having people work at home and building rapid mass transit in the suburbs and new towns,
- establishes a new business and banking model that includes workers as owners in making important decisions, including the distribution of wealth, to dramatically reduce the inequality in society,
- uses the financial resources of government and the private sector to implement solutions to our critical problems at home,
- develops an economic structure serving God and humankind, not a system that rules over us for the pursuit of more money, and
- mobilizes quickly to stop global warming and begin the huge task to replace oil and gasoline, which could be unaffordable or unavailable in thirty years.

The Signs of the Times

The Existential Threat of Global Warming

Without doubt, the worst sign of the times is the "willful ignorance of the powers that be in promoting carbon emissions, presiding over the devastation of large parts of the habitable biosphere, which will not be lost on future generations of those who survive the ongoing calamity." This is an excerpt from an article by Dr. Andrew Glikson, titled "The Arctic Climate Tipping Points: Methane and the Future of the Biosphere,"[1] which points out that the rise in the earth's temperature could melt the permafrost in Alaska, the Canadian Arctic, Siberia, and the Tibetan Plateau, covering nine million square miles. Melting permafrost means potentially releasing vast amounts of methane into the atmosphere. Those who try to deny global warming must read the data and face the realities that scientists have so carefully measured. We must avoid the melting permafrost tipping point.

The International Panel on Climate Change (IPPC) Report, 2018

The IPCC report[2] was written by ninety-one scientists, who reviewed more than six thousand scientific studies. This strong wake-up call fell on deaf ears in the American media. The report concluded that we only have twelve years to limit global warming to 1.5 degrees C.

Climate change is happening at a faster and faster pace, and we are running out of time because the effort required to stop global warming will require a national mobilization that takes decades. The melting of the permafrost is a tipping point that we must try to avoid with great urgency. The IPCC report states that we have now only ten years to reduce CO_2 by 45 percent and avoid destructive climate events.

In order to stop burning fossil fuels that warm the planet, we need to implement renewable energy production and replace oil and gasoline on a mobilization scale never seen before and much faster than during World War II.

The average global temperature has risen 1 degree C since preindustrial times. We have been hammered by Mother Nature, now destroying whole cities and towns, as Hurricane Michael did to Mexico Beach, Florida, and Maria did to Puerto Rico. Wildfires burn out of control in the West, and coastal cities like Miami are already being flooded. Miami, London, New York, and Tokyo are sinking, as shown in the PBS documentary "Sinking Cities".

In the Midwest, crops are hit with drought or are destroyed by too much rainfall, while tons of topsoil are being washed away. New York City cannot protect itself against the rising seas, and we are doing nothing, with no leadership to encourage us to action. We have seen what a 1 degree C rise can do. We do not want to see what 1.5 degrees C can do, let alone the massive devastation of 3.6 degrees C. We have reached the "For Christ's Sake line."

There is hope, however, as we have no choice but to take on the role of Hercules and get to work. This is a human tragedy based on data-driven science. It is not a matter for political debate between Republicans and Democrats. We must end our tribal bickering and unite our hearts, as never before, to fight global warming together.

There are those who speculate that global warming is a weather cycle. It is not, because we have seen carbon dioxide rise since the beginning of industrialization as the direct cause. Moreover, even if this was a climate cycle, we would be insane to make it worse by adding more CO_2 to the atmosphere.

In order to take actions that can bring about a good and safe society, we need to look at the big picture and read the signs of the times with clarity and honesty; then, using a long-range planning framework, we must implement the necessary plans.

Automation and Robots Will Replace Forty-Seven Million Jobs

The Oxford Martin School of Oxford University has forecast that automation can eliminate 50 percent of today's occupations.[3] Corporate forecasters estimate that 30 percent of today's occupations will need to be replaced with other kinds of jobs. Let us assume that at least one-third of our jobs must be replaced. There are currently about 157 million people in the US labor force; 30 percent of 157 million is 47 million new jobs that must be created, at minimum, if we are all to have a livelihood, as opposed to merely having an underpaid job or no livelihood at all.

US Population Projections

According to the US Census Bureau, America's population is expected to grow by an average of 1.8 million people per year between 2017 and 2060. The United States is projected to grow by 78 million people in the next four decades. Livelihoods must be provided for an additional 36 million twenty-year-olds by 2040. We will then need to add 83 million livelihoods by 2040 (47 million, plus 36 million = 83 million). We will need to build affordable energy-efficient homes for this growing population and provide them with a sufficient livelihood. This can best be done by building new towns for the twenty-first century. Our existing cities and towns simply cannot provide the living environment, energy supplies, new technologies, and housing supply that we need. We need to design new towns from scratch.

Definition of a Livelihood

A sufficient livelihood means that people will have enough income or government assistance to have an education and be able to buy a home and have enough income to support a family and have a comfortable retirement with adequate health care, in exchange for a lifetime of work.

We Need a New Business Model and a New Banking Model

This is an enormous national challenge which needs immediate long-range planning by government and the private sector. An economic system that does not provide a good livelihood for all is not worth its salt. We need to distribute the wealth that we all create equitably, not as it is now: 60–90 percent to the investors and owners, and too little to talent and physical labor. As we shall see, this can all be done by design. Establishing a new corporate business model is practical and doable because it has been done successfully, on a regional basis, for over fifty years by the Mondragon Cooperative Corporation, based in Spain. This corporation will be discussed in detail in Chapter 1.

In 2018, the Harvard Joint Center for Housing Studies produced a report titled, "The State of the Nation's Housing."[4] This report states that nearly half of renter households and a quarter of owner households are cost burdened. The Department of Housing and Urban Development defines "housing cost burdened" to be a condition where 30 percent or more of one's income must be spent on housing, which leaves little for groceries, transportation, health care, and other basic needs.

Low-cost rentals have practically disappeared. Salaries have been stagnant for four decades, while housing costs continue to rise. In large metro areas, land is no longer available for affordable housing construction on the scale that it is needed. Housing developers have been permitted by governments to build upscale housing in the $300,000 to $1,000,000 range, which gives developers a larger profit than building affordable housing for the workforce. Across the nation, due to these economic structure imbalances and the lack of federal action, "we are sleep-walking into a national affordable housing crisis," according to the Harvard report. This means that the workforce that includes professions such as teachers, firefighters, and police, and restaurant and hotel workers and those who work in lower-paying jobs, will have to abandon the cities because of the lack of affordable housing. This has already happened in San Francisco, where restaurants are closing down in large numbers. The solution is to build new towns near large cities, with affordable housing, and then build a rapid transit line to the cities so that workers can reach their destination within thirty minutes and then be driven to their workplace in ten-seat vans.

Millions of Employees Need to Work at Home

We need to encourage people to work at home by the millions and cut commuting by moving data rather than moving people. This needs to be done on a massive scale—now, since it will dramatically reduce carbon dioxide emissions. Workers at home can be monitored by quotas, deadlines, and other methods. This must start as soon as possible. Working at home will increase the quality of life and increase productivity.

Oil and Gasoline Could Be Unaffordable or Unavailable by 2040

In a 2010 report, titled *Fueling the Future Forces*,[5] the Department of Defense (DOD) told the armed services that they must be independent of oil within thirty years. This report has subsequently been taken off the internet; however, we will be examining its facts in detail. Subsequent to the DOD report, the United States has added about thirteen years to the deadline for replacing oil with renewable sources by using fracking technology, extending availability to perhaps 2053. However, by about 2040, the world will realize that we are about to run out of oil, and the price will surge to $120–$150 per barrel, which will be unaffordable.

The International Energy Agency's *2010 World Energy Outlook Report* stated that the easy-to-get oil fields will lose 75 percent of their productive capacity by 2035. This report stunned the business world.

Those who deny global warming cannot ignore our need to replace oil with more sustainable energy sources. This is indeed a daunting task that will require immediate and massive national mobilization and the uniting of American society to focus on the projects necessary for success. The alternative is total collapse of our economic system.

One Solution: Building New Towns for the Twenty-First Century

Long-range planning and rapid implementation is required to meet our critical needs for the production of livelihoods, affordable housing, renewable energy, and rapid transit. American government and the private sector have not been good at long-range planning and implementation. The last great American public works project was the interstate highway system. Almost all of these goals, described above, can be achieved by building satellite new towns, comprised of worker-owned and worker-operated corporations, which can supply all the basic necessities of life and a good livelihood for the worker-owners. These proposed new towns can be built with a new manufacturing base that uses automation to replace cheap labor but still supports many workers. They will build energy systems that eliminate carbon dioxide emissions. As MIT Professor Lester Thurow once said, "We can't build an economy by giving each other haircuts. We have to *make* things." To have a national economic structure, we need a strong manufacturing base, which has been shipped overseas for cheap labor for far too long. With automation, we can lower the price of goods and replace much cheap labor with automation. Then, we can buy products produced by the happier American workforce.

The Benefits of Automation Need to Be Enjoyed by All

Around 1980, when we began using computers in business, we were told that we would all share in the wealth created from newfound productivity. Those productivity gains went to investors and owners of corporations; they were not shared with the workers. This time, we will show how the wealth generated from newfound productivity can and should be shared more fairly through new business and banking models.

We Need to Mobilize Now to Address Global Warming

Global warming has already approached tipping points, such as the release of methane on a massive scale in the Arctic and the northern hemisphere. Climate Central is an international team of scientists led by Anders Levermann, who published a study that found "for every degree Fahrenheit of global warming due to carbon pollution, global average sea level will rise about 4.2 feet in the long run. Sea level rise is now growing at about 1 foot per decade. We have two sea levels: the sea level of today, and the far higher sea level that is already being locked in for some distant tomorrow."[6] This means that we must go to a wartime footing in the fight to replace fossil fuels with solar, wind, and safe nuclear energy. Otherwise, New York City, Miami, Seattle, Tokyo, London, and all of the world's coastlines will be overwhelmed by rising sea levels. We will not be able to transport goods on the high seas because the world's ports will be underwater.

You may ask, "Where is the money going to come from to do all of these projects?" Historically, when we needed trillions of dollars to fight a war or reduce taxes on the rich, money magically appeared to meet these purposes. However, when we need to provide decent livelihoods and stop global warming, our leaders balk at making the investment from the national treasury. We need to spend our tax money to create good livelihoods and valuable assets, not for military destruction or to make the rich richer. The billionaire class needs to contribute trillions of dollars to stop global warming and replace gasoline and jet fuel, or they will have no economic system left with which to make more billions. They will be stranded capitalists of their own making. Greed can no longer be the primary value of our economic system. We need to honor the values of truth, goodness, and justice. This is now a matter of survival for the human species.

Stephanie Kelton, a major economist in Washington DC, has made the case that "the basic idea is that the government can't run out of money." She holds "that when people talk about government profligacy bankrupting their grandchildren or triggering a cataclysmic debt crisis, they're conflating the experience of the typical family, which has to get money from somewhere outside the household to meet expenses, with that of a sovereign government, which creates money as part of its basic operation".[7]

When the federal government prints money and spends it on building new towns, new infrastructure, education, sustainable livelihoods, and manufacturing plants, it is creating an ongoing economic structure that produces wealth for investors and pays taxes from a productive workforce. "Eventually, inflation becomes an issue when the amount of money in circulation gets ahead of the productive capacity of the workforce," Kelton concluded. However, she asserted that should not prevent society from using money to meet its positive, productive needs and especially to deal with the existential threats of global warming and the need to replace oil. As we shall see in chapter 8, building new towns for the twenty-first century will pay off all loans borrowed, as happened during the 1930s with the Reconstruction Finance Agency, under President Franklin Roosevelt.

Last year, Adam B. Smith wrote an article citing NOAA's data, which concluded that since 1980, the cumulative costs of 219 climate disasters has exceeded $1.5 trillion.[8] Shall we bury our heads in the rising sea and go for a $5 trillion loss? No, of course not. Let us spend that $5 trillion, and more, on building productive economic assets that provide a good life for all while dealing with destructive global warming. It is time to start reducing our self-inflicted suffering by using our resources to produce something of great value for all, which will last for decades. Most importantly, we can direct our financial resources to solve our critical problems by design and long-range planning. In chapter 8, we discuss several ways to finance the construction of new towns for the twenty-first century.

The Design of a Good Corporation Model

It may come as a surprise to many that better corporate business and banking models can be designed. Pope Francis, in his insightful book, *Encyclical on Climate Change and Inequality*, highlights how the global economic system is flawed:

> "In the meantime, economic powers continue to justify the current global system where priority tends to be given to speculation and pursuit of financial gain, which fail to take the context into account, let alone the effects on human dignity and the natural environment. Here we see how environmental deterioration and human and ethical degradation are closely linked. Many people will deny doing anything wrong because distractions constantly dull our consciousness of just how limited and finite our world really is. As a result, whatever is fragile, like the environment, is defenseless before the interests of a deified market, which become the only rule."[10]

Certainly, we must redesign a global economic system which is destroying the environment with historic flooding, massive forest fires, hurricanes, rising sea levels, and the acidification of the oceans, resulting in $1.5 trillion in damage (so far). Capitalism has been posing that it is a godlike system that cannot be changed. Clearly, if we do not change business as usual, we will all perish; it is an unloving and exceedingly selfish economic system. We really need to design a loving and just economic system that serves all of us. What we need is a system that gives us integral human development, lifting us up to our highest spiritual and economic potential.

Any economic system worth its salt must provide a decent livelihood for everyone. Corporations have been operating not to serve us, but with one goal only: to make more money. To design a worthy business and banking model, we need to start with good values to guide us. We need to base our design on the guiding values of truth, goodness, and justice, all leading to the pursuit of the common good. There are those who will claim that "my values are as good as your values." This is an attempted escape into relativism: Everything is relative, and "I can do just as I like." However, there is a higher authority and guide than human authority. I must appeal to a higher authority: Jesus, who taught the values of truth, goodness, and justice, which, in my opinion, are the values comprising love.

Fortunately, we do not have to design a new business model that embraces these good values from nothing, as it has been done for us in large measure. Most importantly, it has a formula for the distribution of wealth, which gives people their just due and provides everyone with the resources to enjoy financial security and the pursuit of happiness. Our hearts cannot rest in any economic system that does not provide each member with livelihood resources as a right. As cited above, these resources must be enough to raise a family, own a house, and have health care, transportation, electricity, food, education, and a comfortable retirement, in exchange for a lifetime of work. Now that can be accomplished on a national scale and eventually on a global scale.

Chapter 1 will describe a new way of doing business and banking that pays just wages that provide livelihoods. We will describe the most successful worker-owned cooperative in the world, which has been the best-kept secret in economics classes for far too long.

Chapter 1

Worker-Owned Cooperatives: A New Business and Banking Model

We need to build satellite new towns that provide millions of sustainable livelihoods, affordable housing, and large-scale renewable energy production within a new manufacturing base. In order to restore some equality in the distribution of income, worker-owned and worker-governed cooperatives can be developed side-by-side with current businesses. While worker-owned cooperatives will not be for everyone, especially many of the professions, worker-owned cooperatives will be well received by the vast majority of the working people, simply because they give them financial security and a livelihood for life, which has become a challenging global need.

Worker-owned cooperatives can produce all the basic necessities of life in most regions of the world. A complex of regional cooperatives can agree to buy each other's products. Cooperatives can also go outside their region to obtain goods such as seafood or electric automobiles from another cooperative. Regional cooperatives can export 20 percent or more of their products in order to buy luxuries they cannot produce. The major products for local use and export are solar power, wind energy, safe nuclear power, and biofuels, which will be needed to replace oil for decades to come. The most successful cooperative corporation in the world is the Mondragon Cooperative Corporation (MCC).

Mondragon employs 74,335 people as full-time worker-owners. MCC has many manufacturing, construction, food supply, and educational cooperatives. In 2014, Mondragon had 24.72 billion euros in assets and annual revenues of 12 billion euros, according to their annual report.[1] Mondragon has exported advanced technologies to Germany, and as

Mondragon University Professor Fred Freundlich remarked, that "is no small trick in Europe." Mondragon has fifteen technology research divisions. It has technology exchange agreements with General Motors and Microsoft.

They have taken control of their community and their lives. That is true economic and political freedom. Table 1 lists the different sectors formed by MCC in 1987; this shows that worker-owner cooperatives can supply all the basic necessities of life in a regional economic structure.

Table 1
The Number of Cooperatives in Each Sector (1987)

Industrial	86
Educational	46
Housing	15
Agricultural	8
Service Sector	4
Retail	1
Support	6
Total	**166**

Source: Roy Morrison, *We Build the Road as We Travel*.[2]

Clearly, a new workplace platform must be developed as soon as possible by workers and spiritually healthy, good-hearted wealthy individuals for the old workplace platform is sinking and barely holding together. France has already had violent riots in the streets because of the oppressive insecurity established by wealth inequality. Donald Trump was elected mostly by frustrated people who have not seen their stagnant wages meet their needs for forty years. Trump convinced them that he was a businessman and a billionaire who could fix their economic problems. He said, "Only I can fix it." Millions believed him out of desperation. Trump has failed to fix the closing of General Motors plants, which has plans to cut fourteen thousand employees. He cannot control the large corporations. Will his supporters ever see that he lied to them?

Business owners and investors have taken 60–90 percent of the wealth to the owners, investors, and top management. This arrangement cannot stand.

A New and Just Way to Distribute the Wealth that We All Produce

Here is how the profits are divided in Mondragon: All worker-owners are paid a livelihood wage, which means enough for education, owning a home and car, being able to marry and raise a family, and have a comfortable retirement. At the end of the year, after all costs are paid, 70 percent goes to the worker-owner retirement plan, 20 percent goes to a reserve fund to keep the cooperative viable and thriving, and 10 percent goes to the community. The ratio of pay to top managers is 6 to 1, compared to the entry-level employees. MCC does not have stockholders; however, it uses commercial loans along with retirement savings and savings of capital by labor to create new jobs.[3]

MCC has built a model platform that can be replicated around the world. It can be built side-by-side of the existing failing platforms. Mondragon has a presence in ninety-seven countries and sales in 150 countries.

According to Wikipedia, "In 2009, 59.4% of total turnover came from international sales. Sales resulting from the export of products abroad and production generated includes 75 subsidiaries located in 14 different countries: China (13), France (9), Poland (8), Czech Republic (7), Brazil (5), Germany (4), United Kingdom (3), Romania (3), United States (2), Turkey (2), Slovakia (2), India (2), Thailand (1), and Morocco (1). Overall, in 2009, these 75 plants produced goods worth 3.1 billion euros. The corporate industrial park in Kunshan, close to Shanghai, currently houses seven subsidiaries."[4]

Mondragon's Banking System: A New Model

One of the biggest advantages to businesses that sign on to the Mondragon cooperative way of doing business is that they can have access to capital for expansion, training, or simply to survive. As every business knows, making payroll is sometimes difficult. Mondragon broke all the rules when they established their own sustainable community banking system.

The Mondragon bank, Caja Laboral, offers a model of strength for existing cooperatives (small businesses) and refined support for start-up businesses. The Banking Division undertakes the community building and integrative work of the cooperatives. The Mondragon Bank accumulates financial resources from workers' retirement savings and commercial loans. It does not have to pay outside shareholders or face pressure to fire thousands of employees for more profit. It does not gamble on the stock market. The Empresarial Division of the bank utilizes the accumulated worker wealth in pension savings, its reserve fund, and commercial loans to launch sustainable start-ups and expand other businesses. The bank produces a business plan with a start-up and continues to track the success of the business. If there's a problem, they will help the start-up. If there were bad management decisions, the bank can have the general manager transferred to another cooperative. If the start-up needs cash to expand or simply meet payroll, the bank can supply the necessary funds. Worker-owned cooperators do not fire each other. If necessary, workers are transferred to other cooperatives or trained for a new start-up cooperative.

Germany Has a Thousand Co-operative Banks

Germany has 1,116 co-operative banks that are flourishing, according to the *Economist*. "These co-operative banks have come through the financial crisis of 2008 with barely a scratch. They argue that their business model, working for the public or mutual good rather than for shareholders, is well suited to the mixture of households and small companies (known as *Mittelstand*) that they serve. The savings banks and co-operative banks provide about two-thirds of all lending to *Mittelstand* companies and 43 percent of lending to all companies and households."[5]

Elizabeth Warren Proposes that Workers Have a Voice with the Owners

Between 2007 and 2016, large corporations dedicated 60–90 percent of profits to owners and shareholders. Regular employees had no voice in this matter. This explains why there have been stagnant wages for employees for four decades: 60–90 percent of the profits have been paid to investors, top management, and owners. The remaining 10–40 percent is used for stock buybacks, research, planning, inventory, and so on. Employee wages remained stagnant. US Senator Elizabeth Warren has proposed the Federal Accountable Capitalism Act, which would apply to corporations with $1 billion in annual revenue. The bill mandates that a corporation's boards of directors have to be comprised of 40 percent employees. The board would include all major stakeholders, which would include employees, customers, and cities and towns where they operate. This is not Socialism; it is democracy in the workplace. The Socialism or Communist argument just does not apply in this case.

Democratic socialism is essentially defined as using programs run by the government to provide necessary services to the public that the private sector will not or cannot provide, such as Social Security and Medicare.

The Ten Cooperative Principles of Mondragon Cooperatives

Open Admission

The cooperative system is open to all who agree with the basic cooperative principles without regard to ethnic background, religion, political beliefs, or gender.

Democratic Organization

The cooperative system is based on the equality of owner-workers. The cooperative is democratically controlled on the basis of one member, one vote; its governing structures are democratically controlled and are also responsible to the general assembly or elected body.

Sovereignty of Labor

Labor is the essential transformative factor of society. Cooperatives renounce wage labor, give full power to the owner-workers to control the co-ops, give primacy to workers in distribution of surpluses, and work to extend the cooperative choice to all members of society.

Instrumental Character of Capital

Capital is basically accumulated labor resources and a necessary factor in business development and savings. The co-ops pay a just but limited return on capital saved or invested, a return that is not directly tied to the losses or surpluses of the co-ops. Their need for capital shall not impede the principle of open admission, but after an initial trial period, co-op members must make a substantial, affordable, and equal financial investment in the cooperative. At present, this membership contribution is equal to a year's salary of the lowest paid member.

Self-Management

Cooperation involves both collective effort and individual responsibility. Cooperation is the development of the individual, not against others but with others. Democratic control means participation in management and the ongoing development of the skills needed for self-management. There must be clear information available on the co-op's operations, systematic training of owner-workers, internal promotion for management positions, and consultations and negotiations with all cooperators in organizational decisions that affect them.

Pay Solidarity

The co-ops will practice both internal and external pay solidarity. Internally, the total pay differential between the lowest-paid and the highest-paid member shall not exceed a factor of six. In addition, compensation is comparable to that prevailing in neighboring conventional firms.

Group Cooperation

Co-ops are not isolated entities. Cooperation exists on three levels: among individual co-ops organized into groups; among co-op groups; and between the Mondragon system and other movements.

Social Transformation

Cooperation in the Mondragon system is an instrument for social transformation. As Jose Maria Arizmendiarrieta, a founder of the movement, wrote, "Cooperation is the authentic integration of people in the economic and social process that shapes a new social order; the cooperators must make this objective extend to all those who hunger and thirst for justice in the working world."

The cooperatives reinvest a 10 percent portion of their surpluses in the Basque community. A significant portion goes toward new job development, to community development (through the use of social funds), to a social security system based on mutual solidarity and responsibility, and to cooperation with other institutions (such as unions).

Universal Nature

The co-ops proclaim their solidarity with all who labor for economic democracy, peace, justice, human dignity, and development in Europe and elsewhere, particularly with the peoples of the Third World.

Education

Education is essential for fulfilling the basic cooperative principles. It is fundamentally important to devote sufficient human and economic resources to cooperative education, professional training, and general education of young people for the future.

Source: *We Build The Road as We Travel*, by Roy Morrison[6]

The Mondragon Cooperative Corporation Is Not Socialism or Communism

A brief review of the tenets of Fascism, Socialism, and Communism will show how it differs from the tenets of Mondragon. In Fascism, Socialism, and Communism, economic and political power is concentrated in the hands of a few, a governing elite, which is a bureaucratic body of state government control. It denies freedom and independence of the individual. It is non-Christian. It is an atheistic and materialistic system, which demands absolute dependency of all citizens on the state for their income security and well-being. Prices and wages are controlled by the state. Citizens are under the control of the government with the armed services and police power. No wonder that such an unjust and uncaring system cannot survive. Under capitalism, we experience much of the same results, with control of the political system by the billionaire class, pursuing and serving money only. How long can this economic system last without addressing its many flaws? Clearly, we have reached the hour of transformation.

We Are Being Put to the Final Test

It has to be said and said plainly: Earth is being destroyed before our eyes by our own actions because we have been serving money and not God. God sent his Son to us to give us instructions on how to have a good life, filled with love, beauty, and peace. Christ said, "No one can serve two masters. He will either hate one and love the other, or be devoted to one and despise the other. You cannot serve God and mammon" (Matthew 6:24).

The love and pursuit of money is the only goal within the charter of large corporations. They claim to have one fiduciary responsibility: making more money. They have no other expressed values, such as protecting nature and the environment that supports our ecosystems and our very lives. I must conclude that this is ruining God's beautiful creation and our own lives at the same time. In order to survive, we will need to change our minds according to Christ's teachings or perish by our own hands. This is our final test. God gave us free will, and he gave us instructions for operating the Spaceship Earth: Christ's teachings. Shall we unite and work together for the good of humankind, to protect and nurture God's creation? Or shall we perish by our own hands?

The Mondragon corporate model places job creation as its first priority; making money is second. The distribution of wealth is held to a moderate level at a ratio of 6 to 1, based on the entry-level salary. Money is set aside for a comfortable retirement; 10 percent of profits go to the community as a whole for the benefit of all. In Mondragon, you will not find mansions on the hill, but rather, everyone has affordable housing and all the appliances needed to raise a family. Consumption of goods in Mondragon is sufficient but not lavish or pretentious. The people are happy and at peace. This is a model that enables us to serve God and not just money. That is why it succeeds and gives all a good life. This corporate model has competed in the market, successfully, for over fifty years.

The Western lifestyle has been drawn into overconsumption, which scientists tell us is unsustainable for us and the whole world. We can change our lifestyle and still thrive. We can live our lives based on the universal, transcendent values of truth, goodness, justice, and beauty, which are the values needed to save ourselves and the beautiful planet earth.

Mondragon's Economic Ladder

Allecoop is a special cooperative in Mondragon that provides an economic ladder for young people. It is described in Roy Morrison's excellent book on Mondragon, *We Build the Road as We Travel*. Young people are given jobs to assemble electrical components, wiring modules for household appliances, and electrical wiring for vehicles. Manufacturing cooperatives farm these tasks out to Allecoop, and they pay enough to enable youths to work their way through college, while getting vocational training. This unique co-op factory is largely run by students.

Ronald Reagan Advocated for Worker-Owned Cooperatives

In the first half of the twentieth century, the federal government passed enabling legislation for farmer co-ops, credit unions, and rural electric companies. With the help of Republicans and Democrats in Congress, employee ownership flourished in companies such as Southwest Airlines, Publix Super Markets (now owners of a thousand supermarkets), Ace Hardware, and Land O' Lakes dairy products. Reagan gave a speech where he described worker-owned cooperatives as a logical development of democracy. It brings democracy to the workplace. Most notably, it also provides for more wealth equality in the workplace without raising taxes on the rich. Reagan said, "When workers have a stake in the place where they work, they have a stake in the freedom of their country. In the U.S., employee ownership is a path that benefits a free people."

A Secure and Just Place to Work

The Mondragon formula for the distribution of wealth produced by all provides a living wage for a broad middle class. Clearly, a well-functioning economic system requires a broad middle class in order to have people who earn enough to buy what we produce. If the so-called elite take all the money to the top, the middle class is decimated. How have they missed this critical economic requirement? According to Compustat, in 2017, the payouts to corporate shareholders was 72 percent. When you add on the amount that goes to the owners and top management, 90 percent of the profits go to the top, with little left for wages of the workers who actually produced the profits. This immoral system is called "wage stealing."

Mondragon's elimination of the conflict between capital and labor is a major victory for integral human development. Mondragon workers receive a just living wage and a safe and secure place to work. Regional cooperatives produce the basic necessities of life; this is doable, and Mondragon has been doing it for over fifty years.

Worker-owners do not like to fire each other. In MCC, if there is a problem, worker-owners are shifted to another cooperative or retrained. They value job security. American corporations often fire thousands of people at one time, leaving them to find another job to survive (usually, not a job that pays the same). That is no way to run an economic system.

Chapter 2 will describe how the construction of new towns for the twenty-first century, on a large scale, will provide an answer to our most critical needs.

Chapter 2
The Creation of New Towns for the Twenty-First Century

How to Develop Regional Complexes of Worker-Owner Cooperatives

A complex of several cooperatives can be built near existing cities and towns, built to provide all the basic necessities of life. The ideal process will be to build Mondragon-style cooperatives within a new town planning framework. This framework will enable the planners, architects, engineers, and small farmers to take full advantage of our sustainable development ideas and techniques. It can include our best practices in recycling waste and precious materials used in manufacturing. It will include sustainable, regenerative agriculture and sustainable development. It can eliminate fossil fuel burning and oil spills, which are polluting our drinking water and our oceans. It will be an economic model for providing the nation with the basic necessities of life. Most importantly, it can provide affordable housing for the workforce.

Many American Cities Are Unaffordable for the Workforce

The Joint Center for Housing Studies at Harvard University report, "The State of the Nation's Housing 2018,"[1] said, "If America's largest cities, where job growth has been concentrating for years, can't offer anything beyond check-to-check living, the entire country is sleepwalking into a crisis." For decades, America's housing developers have been building upscale housing and McMansions costing $200,000 to $1,000,000, because they are the most profitable to build. Even if the government chose to subsidize working people's housing, there is not enough inexpensive land to build

11

upon in most cities. The solution is to build satellite new towns with high-speed rapid transit lines to the central city, with vans to drive people to their workplaces. Satellite new towns offer the best solution to a housing crisis in the making, by providing new jobs and a way to provide for the largest cities to have a workforce. Let us recall that the workforce includes teachers, police officers, firefighters, salespeople, and restaurant workers. We can't live well without their services, and they cannot serve us if they can't afford housing and a decent life. How obvious can this situation be? And how disgusting?

Steps to Building New Towns of the Twenty-First Century

The first step in building a new town is to have leaders form a group of urban and regional planners, geologists, architects, engineers, renewable energy developers, financiers, and agriculture experts. This planning conference group would select the most inviting regions to demonstrate new towns. These regions will have adequate water supplies for the present and future. The new town sites would build solar, wind, safe nuclear power, and biofuel systems, in order to rapidly replace oil and gasoline over the next thirty years.

Universities in the area would then be invited to join this exciting endeavor, along with existing cooperatives in the region. Ohio and the Rust Belt are prime candidates for this dynamic job-creation project. The states with the most wind power, from Texas to North Dakota, would also be selected.

The second step would be to have a team visit the Otalora Management Training Center in Mondragon. They would learn how to start and operate cooperatives, with instruction in finance, distribution, and industrial issues. The third step will be to arrange for financing.

Public Sector Investment (See Chapter 8)

The federal government needs to create a Department of Sustainable Job Creation, with a mission of creating eighty-three million livelihoods, over the next thirty years. This should be a cabinet-level department with annual funding equal to that of the Department of Defense: $700 billion. You may ask, "Where will the money come from?" As described above, one answer has been provided by economist Stephanie Kelton, who determined that "the government cannot run out of money. It creates money just by spending."[2]

For example, if the government prints money and spends that money to create a new manufacturing base with robots and automation, it will create physical assets and sustainable jobs, and it will produce much wealth for decades. Can these new manufacturing jobs compete with foreign businesses that use slave labor? With new automation technology that eliminates cheap labor, they could. America doesn't have to compete on price, as long as Americans buy what is made here, thereby giving security to their own jobs while rebuilding the economy's manufacturing structure.

Also, military spending is extremely bloated, and the DOD's budget needs to be dramatically reduced, along with arms sales, since the only thing they can be used for is the destruction of lives, homes, and infrastructure. The United States should return to its moral values and not engage in making money from arms sales. We have more ethical and beneficent ways to make money.

The DOD cannot even account to Congress for all they spend on nonproductive assets. We certainly need a strong defense, but the strongest defense is needed in the cyber warfare field, not unnecessary, costly, and unsustainable ground wars, as former secretary of defense Robert Gates declared at West Point Military Academy on February 25, 2011. We must avoid large land wars in order to have resources to deal with global warming and our own livelihoods.

Private Sector Investment

In 2018, an alliance of institutional investors with $22.5 trillion under management encouraged governments to shift resources to deal with climate change, claiming it creates too much risk for investors. It is just too disruptive and risky for a stable business and institutional environment. In December 2018, a group of 414 institutional investors with $31 trillion under management said governments must take serious steps to cut emissions.[3]

Large corporations need to invest wealth that is created by automation in a massive job creation program. After all, eighty-three million livelihoods by 2040 is a big hole to fill. Corporations will need a new charter to distribute the wealth to all who produce it. We suppose that they will yell, "Socialism!" No, what we are talking about is just some reasonable level of equality in the distribution of the profits that we produce. In fact, Socialism and Communism are atheistic systems which give the state and a group of the elite control over the people with police power. In contrast, what in fact we are describing here are rules for social justice and democracy in the workplace, in the form of Christian worker-owned corporations that share the wealth. The anti-Socialist argument does not apply here. We need to learn how to love and care for one another in the economic system if we are to survive at all.

Chapter 8 discusses the need to institute public banks; we need to prevent the collapse of the current financial system. Public banks could also be the main source for financing the new town's infrastructure and renewable energy production.

The fourth step would be to write an open letter to the billionaires of the world, offering them the golden opportunity to finance the new towns and provide renewable energy before oil becomes unaffordable or unavailable. More than a hundred billionaires, led by Bill Gates and Warren Buffet, have already committed to donate half their money to philanthropic causes. Organizers could also send letters to the approximately 2,208 billionaires in the world, with an invitation to participate in building a sustainable economic system. The new town projects would only need about five billionaires to begin building a series of new towns that can solve the nation's most critical problems.

To finance this project, including purchasing land and building infrastructure, the billionaires would be invited to join the government and the planning team to offer their knowledge and expertise. Many billionaires are deeply concerned about the potential loss of 50 percent of livelihoods due to the oncoming march of robots, information technology, and software programs. The new town projects can provide these morally conscious billionaires with a way out of the oncoming economic turmoil and violent riots in the streets, as we have seen with the yellow jackets in France.

Also, as described above, the federal and state governments have a big job to do by building the infrastructure for satellite new towns, providing affordable, solar-powered, energy-efficient housing for working families.

Purchasing Land for Twenty-First-Century New Towns

With financing in place by the government and private sector, the fifth step would be to purchase large tracts of land within the chosen regions, which would be largely agricultural or unproductive land. First, landowners would be offered the appraisal price plus 25 percent for their land. If that offer was not accepted, they could be offered stock in the whole new town enterprise. If those offers fail, the federal government or the state would need to use eminent domain, which would still offer landowners just compensation. The rationale for using eminent domain would be for the national interest and national security, given the existential needs to stop global warming and replace oil as soon as possible. We are, after all, in crisis mode. Greed has to make concessions for our survival, reducing economic uncertainty, and increasing the potential for financial security of all, not just a few.

With new town planning, there would be many jobs created in the chosen region. They would include a new rapid transit system; technology parks to produce solar, wind, nuclear, and biofuels; a new electricity grid; and safe thorium-fueled nuclear reactors.

Robots and technology management would be used liberally, since the profits would be returned to the worker-owners who build and operate these systems. This project will lead the job creation program. Building new towns with affordable housing will create millions of jobs and work for unskilled laborers. The Harvard Joint Center of Housing Studies has reported that housing and housing-related industries create 25 percent of the jobs in the economy. The author has verified this report by a detailed study of occupation statistics.

Laminated Glue Wood-Frame High-Rises

Architects will need to build high-rise apartments and condos in order to save land for agriculture. Lever Architecture Company in Portland, Oregon, is managing the construction of a twelve-story high-rise with laminated glue wood beams and columns. It is necessary to shift away from concrete and steel construction as much as possible because it releases too much carbon dioxide into the atmosphere. As always, wood is good. This will also create thousands of jobs in forestry for planting millions of trees as a carbon sink and then for construction.

15

Billionaires Will Invest in New Town Construction

The construction of new towns to meet our critical needs would give the participating billionaires a new purpose in life and a nationally praised legacy. On *60 Minutes*, billionaire Ray Dalios expressed his desire to correct some of the major flaws of the current economic system by rebuilding the middle class. Dalios said that the wealth gap has become too large: "We are at a juncture which can lead to conflict between the rich and the poor." He said he believes "that capitalism needs to be reformed, not abandoned." He would like to see "the best ideas win." He has offered half of his $18 billion to solve our critical problems.

Dalios, the Koch brothers, Warren Buffet, Bill and Linda Gates, Elon Musk, the Walton family, Mark Zuckerberg, and Jeff Bezos are all invited to build new towns for the twenty-first century. We need to establish financial security for families if we want a good and productive and loving society. How obvious can that be?

The sixth step is to establish a Mondragon-style banking system. An MCC-style bank accepts large amounts of capital from private investors and pays them a good return on investment from the sale of products and renewable energy. To my knowledge, Mondragon has not done this on a large scale. However, the Mondragon bank does accept outside commercial loans without being burdened by stockholders. A governmental reconstruction finance agency can be created to do the same thing (see chapter 8).

Capitalist corporations reportedly pay out 90 percent of profits to investors and owners, according to an article by Harold Meyerson, "In Corporations, It's Owner Take All."[4] Investors in Mondragon worker-owner cooperatives need to have good will and accept Christ's social teaching to avoid egoistic conflicts in regards to managing and funding the enterprise. Investors need to accept that sustainable job creation is the top priority rather than making more profits. The whole operation may well benefit from having progressive spiritual leaders to provide leadership and conflict resolution.

A seventh step would be to build renewable energy technology parks using solar, wind, safe nuclear energy, and the latest biofuel technology to produce large quantities of energy for local use and for sale to other regions. The aviation industry needs large quantities of biofuel to replace jet fuel. Clearly, the nation must start to limit the number of commercial airline flights that are flown.

Yes, we can make some sacrifices for the sake of our children's future. The National Air Traffic Controllers Association report that there are over eighty-seven thousand flights crisscrossing the United States every day, half of them on passenger airlines. Much of this air traffic is for shipping goods. Clearly, the consumer society has gotten out of hand by reducing people to consumers to find their joys in life. They are using airline and truck delivery instead of going to the local store.

Biofuels such as ethanol cause fewer greenhouse gas emissions in comparison to oil and gasoline, since biofuels are produced from plants which take in carbon dioxide. Since oil is projected by the Department of Defense to be unaffordable or unavailable by 2040, we have little choice but to shift to producing massive amounts of biofuels as soon as possible.

Renewable energy production would be a primary means of creating wealth for the new towns. Outside grants and loans would be the fastest way to build a regional complex of cooperatives. If only a few multibillionaires chose to invest in such a planned regional complex, a very exciting model could be constructed in a few years. This would show the nations how to grow with renewable energy and a sustainable economic model in a comprehensive planning fashion.

Solar, Wind, Nuclear, Biofuels: The Major Products of the Cooperatives

The new town projects would build large-scale facilities to produce wind, solar, nuclear power, and biofuels for local use and export. The region would also perfect the construction of a new secure electricity grid, safe from computer hackers, as a model for the nation.

Again, Mondragon is a successful regional project, so it is practical and doable. The development of such a Mondragon-style, regional economic model would truly advance humankind. It would demonstrate how to stop warring and start evolving to a better future for the entire world. The financiers and bankers who launch the new town projects would be richly rewarded by society's praise as well as gaining economically and avoiding the collapse of our economic system.

As cited above, the new town projects would fully utilize the talents of planners, architects, engineers, financiers, and other professionals. The design can be done in order to conserve energy and reduce the cost of transportation and the overall cost of living.

Land use planners would determine the most suitable arrangement of sites for residential, commercial, and industrial facilities and set aside land for agriculture and recreation. Then, a new surface rapid transit system would be designed onto which all of the land uses would then be actually built. With such a system, similar to the highly successful system in Curitiba, Brazil, everyone would have access to workplaces, shopping, schools and universities, churches, entertainment, and recreation. By design, this transit system would enable families to own only one car for emergencies and long-distance driving, saving as much as eight thousand to sixteen thousand dollars per year per family. The transit system would be designed so as to allow future expansion, but only within sustainable development limits, to be established by the planners. Self-driving autonomous vehicles (AVs) can reduce the amount of parking dramatically, by circulating around the new town, picking up and dropping off customers at very low prices. Planners will not have to build huge parking lots, freeing up more than 30 percent of the land for better land uses. At night, AVs can be parked under huge arrays of solar cells on the perimeter of the new town.

The transit system would be a bus system, much like Marta in Atlanta or the Washington DC Metro. However, the system would use renewable energy and vehicles, operating above ground on dedicated traffic lanes. People would purchase tickets and queue up at station platforms with short waiting times. Also, driverless cars can have dedicated traffic lanes as well, since they operate with an abundance of caution and can slow down traffic.

The New Town Planning Framework

The new towns would be constructed within a forty-minute travel distance on a high-speed rapid transit line to a major city that needs affordable housing for their workforce. In some cases, this may require vehicles to travel at 80–100 miles per hour on dedicated lanes.

The Harvard report cited above notes that "if America's biggest cities, where job growth has been concentrating for years, can't offer anything beyond check-to-check living, the entire country is sleepwalking into a crisis."

Time is of the essence, for the whole nation is running out of time to provide affordable housing for the workforce and to provide enough income to support a decent family life. However, now we have the physical problem of providing affordable housing as well. There is a limited amount of land within driving distance of our major cities on which to build affordable housing. A high-speed rapid transit system appears to be a viable answer, coupled to affordable housing in the satellite new towns.

Politicians and the corporate decision makers in America are going to have to provide for the labor force, or the largest cities will sleepwalk into a very limited available workforce.

Regional Cooperatives Can Have More Control over Supply and Pricing

When cooperatives are built to serve two hundred to five hundred thousand people, prices can be controlled in a given region when a complex of cooperatives have mutual agreements. For example, if an Asian manufacturer sells a refrigerator for fifty dollars less than the cooperative can produce it, the cooperators can meet and agree not to buy the Asian model, because if they do, they know that they will have to transfer as many as two thousand cooperators to new cooperatives. They can simply say no to global competitors, especially to those who do not pay a living wage to their workers; this provides money to corporations to make their product more affordable than the rest of the global market. The cooperators can make the decision not to buy the cheaper product by democratic vote. This is making the choice that money doesn't mean everything; living a good and secure life is more important for the whole community.

Global Gifts of Wealth Are Guiding Integral Human Development

The wealth of nations increased dramatically with the invention of the steam engine. When nations shifted from coal to oil, their wealth increased again with the rise of the automobile, airplanes, trucks, and expressways to advance commerce and create jobs. Now, we are poised to increase the wealth of all nations again, with the use of superabundant renewable and clean energy: solar, wind, and safe nuclear power. After the construction of energy farms, the wind and the sun are free. When the sun does not shine and the wind does not blow, safe thorium-fueled molten salt nuclear mini-reactors will work 24/7 to supply electricity to the grid.

The renewable energy age will provide inexpensive energy in huge quantities, providing a global gift of wealth and the creation of livelihoods for all with a living wage, but only within a cooperative economic system that knows how to distribute wealth equitably, through cooperation and sharing. Once freed from the destruction of the earth by burning fossil fuels, we can produce an abundance of goods and services at lower actual cost. We will still be limited in growth by the amount of natural resources we use and recycle, so our new economies will need to implement efficient recycling processes, as recommended by scientists who track the limits to growth. We must also create synthetic resources and new materials for use in manufacturing. Plastics must be biodegradable or eliminated outright, for they are destroying life in the ocean.

The Limits to Growth

In its first report, published in 1972, the Limits to Growth,[5] a scientific team working at Massachusetts Institute of Technology (MIT), predicted that the limited availability of mined natural resources relative to rising costs would slow continued economic growth by around the middle of the twenty-first century (i.e., 2050).

This was reported in the *Guardian* article "Scientists Vindicate 'Limits to Growth'—Urge Investment in 'Circular Economy.'" The *Guardian* article by Graham Turner and Cathy Alexander, published on September 1, 2014, further reported that in 2008, CSIRO, Australia's scientific research agency, concluded that the Limits to Growth forecast of potential "global ecological and economic collapse coming up in the middle of the 21st century" due to convergence of "peak oil, climate change, and food and water security" is "on track." Actual current trends in these areas "resonate strongly with the overshoot and collapse model displayed in the book's business-as-usual scenario." "Limits to economic growth, or even de-growth," the report says, do not imply an end to prosperity but rather a conscious decision by societies to lower their environmental impact, reduce wasteful consumption, and increase efficiency, changes which could in fact increase the quality of life. Research needs to be conducted into how to create advanced materials for manufacturing processes. Constructing new towns will require enormous amounts of electricity, so we will need to construct solar farms and wind farms and especially nuclear power on a massive scale *before* building them; once in place, new towns will produce even more renewable energy.

Liquid Fluoride Thorium Reactors

Richard Martin, in his book *Super Fuel: Thorium, the Green Energy Source for the Future,*[6] makes a strong case for the rapid scaling up of safe liquid fluoride thorium mini-reactors to produce electrical energy around the clock. He holds that we need this low-cost energy source, which can be assembled quickly in multiple plants and shipped to different regions. Once they are approved for safety, LFTRs can be scaled up faster than solar, wind, or biofuels. Also known as molten salt reactors, these mini-nuclear reactors produce between 250 and 400 megawatts (the salt is used for cooling). They are not like the huge old uranium reactors that are subject to meltdowns and can spread radioactivity over a wide area.

We need to do a global risk analysis, because we cannot afford the destruction of 1.5 degrees C of global warming, yet alone 2.0 degrees C. We need to have a model that is far less risky than total economic system collapse in 2040–2050.

These small mini-reactors, producing 250–400 megawatts each, are inherently safe—unlike large, conventional nuclear reactors.

Here are a list of pros and cons of using LFTRs for our consideration.

Pros

- Liquid fluoride thorium reactors are carbon-free.
- They are far safer than conventional light water reactors.
- There is abundant fuel (thorium). The International Nuclear Energy Agency estimates the United States has 440,000 tons of thorium reserves. As a nuclear fuel, thorium reserves carry enough energy to power humanity's machines for many millennia into the future. About 1,650 tons of thorium would satisfy all of the electricity needs of the entire world for a whole year at this writing in 2019.

- It is currently being developed in China, Canada, and the United States by companies like Flibe and Terrestrial Energy.
- It generates very small amounts of low-level radioactive waste, which can be buried in deep, safe, geologic depositories.
- It requires far less land than solar.
- It runs around the clock, providing electric power day and night.
- Thorium is far less suitable for weapons proliferation than conventional nuclear fuel. It would be virtually impossible to obtain weapon-grade fuel.
- It is relatively low cost and scalable. We have so little time. 250- to 400-megawatt machines can be mass-produced in manufacturing plants and transported in containers by truck to new towns.
- It requires less cooling water than conventional reactors and can use water from inland ponds.
- LFTRs can refine existing nuclear waste into LFTR by-products.
- The cost of electricity from LFTRs was estimated at 3.8 cents per kilowatt-hour.

Cons

- It still produces hazardous waste (though far less) and radiation drops off much faster.
- Technology and construction would need to be accelerated dramatically, to 2025 or 2030.
- The fuel is non-renewable.

(Adapted from R P Siegel, *Liquid Fluoride Thorium Power: Pros and Cons.*)

On May 4, 2012, Richard Martin, a main proponent of FLTRs, was interviewed by Ira Flatow on the NPR radio show *Science Friday*. Martin talked about the safety factor. He said, "In order to build a bomb with uranium-233, you somehow have to obtain it out of the reactor. And because this is a self-contained, liquid fuel system, there is no point at which you can divert the material. There is no material sitting around in a warehouse somewhere, getting ready to be put in the reactor and so on. And in order to obtain that material, you would have to somehow breach the reactor, shut it down, separate out the fissionable material and get away with it. And as I say in *Super Fuel*, the book, good luck with that. But the other point is that even if you did manage to do that, the uranium-233 is contaminated with yet another isotope, U-232, which is one of the nastiest substances in the universe, and it makes handling and processing and separation out the U-233 virtually impossible, even for a sophisticated nuclear power lab, much less a rogue nation, or terrorist group or someone of that ilk."[6]

Scaling up the LFTRs to 1,500 Gigawatts by 2040

In 2018, the total US electricity-generating capacity was about 1,000 gigawatts. By 2040, we will need at least 1,500 gigawatts to accommodate the nation's growing population, at minimum. Providing electricity for autos, trucks, and buses will require much more.

Richard Martin offers the following scenario for scaling up the LFTRs to 500 gigawatts. One of the beauties of LFTRs is that they can be mass-produced. Small modular LFTRs can be built as 250-megawatt machines and be assembled in large plants. If we build, say, four LFTR plants a year, with each plant producing twenty 250-megawatt reactors, that would just about do it.

Martin estimates the cost of building twenty-four hundred 250-megawatt machines would come to $600 billion. That would produce 600 gigawatts. Add 15 percent for start-up costs and financing, and it rounds up to $700 billion, which is the cost for the US Department of Defense for one year.

If we find that we are not scaling up solar and wind power fast enough to significantly slow down global warming, we can build more production plants for 250-megawatt LFTRs and ship them around the country. We have a way to reduce our anxiety about the adequate supply of zero carbon energy for the future. Nuclear reactors provide electricity 24/7 when the sun doesn't shine and the wind doesn't blow, which solves the electrical storage problem. Those capabilities are worth our time and money.

Martin says, "The president should order the NRC to expedite its licensing process so that the period from application to final approval is no more than five years…. While that process is proceeding, the suppliers to the LFTR production plants can have five years to be ready to supply the plants with finely engineered parts for assembly. That means that while a prototype LFTR is being built (at Savannah River Site, Idaho National Laboratory, or Oak Ridge) companies will begin submitting applications." Please read *Super Fuel: Thorium the Green Energy Source for the Future*, by Richard Martin, for further details.

Terrestrial Energy Company of Canada has an early regulatory review process which is likely on track to commission the first Molten Salt LFTR reactor in North America. The United States needs to invite Terrestrial Energy to America to speed up approval of their technology for implementation in America and the development of plants to produce thousands of these Molten Salt Reactors as soon as possible. Terrestrial Energy is on track to have operational plants in the late 2020s in North America. We need to speed up that process in Canada and the United States.

We have been proposing new designs for our economic system, which focuses on sharing rather than competition. Let us examine some the benefits that can be derived from sharing our wealth in a new and happier society.

What Can Happen When We Share the Wealth of Our Nation

America needs a positive project today that will give us all the opportunity to work together, overcome our political and economic divisions and provide the vision of a much better future for all. In order to stop destructive climate change and build a better economic system, we will need to unite and attack these problems, knowing that our lives and our children's future lives depend on our success. We will have to achieve a greater productive capacity than we did during World War II. Otherwise, the future tribulations of destruction are too horrible to contemplate.

Benefits that Can Flow from a Sharing Economic System

Social consciousness could reach a higher level, wherein it would be easier to cooperate and share instead of competing and being egotistic, selfish, and fearful. We will need to examine dualistic thinking, which sets up conflicts between tribes, like Democrats and Republicans, whites and blacks. We need to move beyond tribal thinking and create a united America, looking out for the benefit of all.

- **A four-day workweek.** Human dignity requires everyone to have the right to work. A four-day workweek would provide enough jobs for all. Slackers will be judged by peers in a worker-owner arrangement. However, in a sense, we will all be slackers, enjoying a four-day workweek. This will be enabled by advances in technologies and computerization, whose productivity benefits can be distributed to all, because Mondragon-style economics distributes wealth to all. People who want to make more money will have three days to dedicate to that purpose, or they can go into the professions, lawyers, doctors, entertainment, or other occupations. Worker-owner cooperatives will not be for everyone, but they will be beneficial to the vast majority of working people, who yearn for financial security and peace of mind, especially in retirement.

- **More family time.** Parents will have more time to spend with their children, who will benefit greatly from the love they receive, which will produce a better society. This is important to create an exponential leap in social consciousness. "Love is contagious," as the song says.

- **Free education**, as is done in several European countries, will be essential to achieve sufficient levels of productivity and creativity in the entire economic system. This will more than pay for itself, as was shown by the GI Bill after World War II. The federal investment returned federal taxes far above the investment from taxpayer dollars, which paid for the college educations of millions of veterans.

- **National health care** would be single-payer or Medicare for all, as is done in many developed economies and is enjoyed by their people at lower cost than in the United States. Profit-making in health care is just a bad idea, because it raises costs by an estimated 15 percent.

- **A dramatic decrease in abortions.** The number one reason for abortions is that women feel they will not have enough income to feed and care for a child. Another related reason is "poor timing." With widespread family income at a middle class level and men employed, we will see abortions dramatically reduced, if not eliminated. Also, the invention of Natural Cycles, an app which can determine a woman's most fertile period, should be able to give most families a means of family planning that they can afford. The failure rate where users become pregnant is 6.9 out of 100; it is not a 100 percent contraceptive, but it can dramatically reduce the number of unwanted pregnancies and abortions.

Charitable organizations and Planned Parenthood can provide access to this app for all who need to plan their family. If a woman cannot afford a cell phone, she can go to a nonprofit to use their phone, take their temperature, and determine the six days when they are going to be fertile. If a family cannot afford to support a child for twenty-five years, they can restrain from unprotected sex for a six-day period. Goodbye to *Roe vs. Wade*. No problem.

- **The end of homelessness.** With a sharing economic structure, poverty and homelessness will be a rarity. Homelessness is a national disgrace that has been shoved under the carpet, out of mind, and out of consideration for legislation. This is an economic catastrophe.
- **Less crime.** When we share the wealth, we will have a dramatic decrease in crime and stealing. Fewer people will have a reason to steal or commit other crimes, as they can be gainfully employed.
- **Less advertising.** With worker-owned cooperatives, we can eliminate spending $500 billion per year on advertising, because most markets will have no competition. Occasionally, there will be an announcement of a new product that will benefit society. Television will be much more enjoyable to watch without being pummeled by people yelling, "Buy my stuff!"
- **Harmony among people.** The spirit of cooperation and sharing would become the norm under such a spiritually enlightened system, which would gradually reduce the selfishness of the ego, which is insidious. Ego impedes the advancement of caring and justice in human relations and governing. In a sharing economy, divisions and polarization would be nearly eliminated, and there would be a newfound harmony among people. We would not blame others for our financial problems or create divisive conspiracy theories.
- **The sharing economy** will work because everyone will be making enough money to have a good livelihood and a comfortable retirement.

- **The sharing economy** will be designed from scratch to give our children and their children a future instead of total economic system collapse.
- **Conflict transcendence.** The ancient, destructive conflict between capital and labor would be eliminated and transcended; in cooperatives, the workers are also the owners. This eliminates the divisive rich-versus-poor ego structure and dualistic thinking of "me versus them."
- **Shared inventions.** The cooperatives can sign agreements to buy each other's products and services. New inventions and improvements in manufacturing technology would be shared by cooperative members, thereby reducing the need for destructive competition and proprietary special interests. Individuals who invent or create, to the benefit of all, would be rewarded financially and publicly.
- **A new age of understanding.** Given a new understanding of balance between individual self-interest and the needs of the whole, the war between conservatives and liberals could be dramatically diminished or eliminated, and then, a new age of political cooperation could begin in government as well as in the business world.
- **Safety net.** There will always be a safety net requirement in any civilized society to take care of the physically and mentally disabled, the frail, and the elderly. However, in a sharing economy, it would cost much less.
- **No utopia.** We will not create a heaven on earth; heaven will be so much more awesome, beyond our imaginations. However, we can "have life and have it more abundantly" on earth and enjoy this life much more. We can do it by designing and implementing a revised economic system.

We need to look through the lens of cooperation and sharing, and eliminate destructive competition. Competition can still be appreciated in the athletic arena, where it belongs.

The next chapter will discuss why we must end our dependence on oil before it becomes unaffordable or unavailable in the next thirty years, as predicted by the Department of Defense.

Chapter 3

Oil Will Be Unaffordable in Thirty Years

The Pentagon Leads the Way for a Shift from Oil to Solar Energy and Biofuels

The Pentagon has announced that the military must be supplied by other energy sources than oil within the next thirty years, because the price and availability of oil cannot be guaranteed. These facts were published on September 27, 2010, in a report from the Department of Defense to the military, titled *The Joint Operating Environment 2010—Joint Forces Command*.[1] This report is a long-range planning assessment of critical factors that will impact the operational capability of the military over the next thirty years. A second report, *Fueling the Future Force*, by Christine Parthemore and John Nagl, was published on September 27, 2010, by the Center for a New American Security.[2]

This report claims that military branches must be independent of oil within thirty years. While fracking has increased America's oil supply, it may only last ten years. Also, the recent discovery of a deposit of twenty billion barrels of oil in West Texas will only gain three years. This would push the timetable to 2053. However, by 2040, when the whole world sees we are running out of oil, the price of oil will skyrocket and be unaffordable for people who drive gas-powered cars.

Scientists have determined that we will need to leave much of the oil that is available in the ground, in order to reduce deadly carbon emissions and global warming. Furthermore, due to solar and wind being so low in cost, energy companies are now shifting investments from oil to renewable energy (although the pace is far too slow).

John Nagl also wrote a book on counter-insurgency in Iraq, which indicates that this Pentagon report was widely read by President Obama and leading policymakers. We need to elect leaders who care about the nation and will strive for solutions to meet the future energy needs of the domestic economy as well as the military.

The Military and the Domestic Economy Must Be Independent of Oil by 2040

Fracking technology may have added thirteen years to our oil supply; however, we can no longer control our oil supply from the Middle East. Another war in the region, for example, with Iran, could reduce our national energy supply by ten or more years. In 2017, we imported 10.1 million barrels of oil per day, from eighty-four countries, according to the US Energy Information Agency. We may have gained much from fracking, but we are still an oil-importing nation.

OPEC countries provided 33 percent and Canada provided 40 percent of the oil imported by the United States. However, as we shall see, our supply of easy-to-get oil is on the decline, and it needs to be replaced by renewable energy.

This coming energy crisis sets the stage for the United States to transform itself in many positive ways. There needs to be a full-blown global consciousness that ensuring the survival of the planet, promoting human safety, and developing sustainable livelihood systems for families are far more critical than any military venture.

Defense planners have already concluded that the military itself must be completely independent of oil in thirty years. This point was constantly brought home in *Fueling the Future Force*. The report was done by a national security and defense think tank based in Washington DC, which had political connections to the Obama White House, with several former employees being picked for key posts by the Obama administration. In fact, a 2009 opinion piece in the *Washington Post* stated, "In the era of Obama ... the Center for a New American Security may emerge as Washington's go-to think tank on military affairs." As stated above, it is clear that the Obama administration was aware of these issues and implemented a plan of action for the military to transition from oil to solar, wind, and other energy sources. Yet Congress is still giving billions of dollars in subsidies to the oil industry, apparently in exchange for campaign contributions.

The denial of global warming by the Trump administration and the

Republican Congress's lack of action in promoting renewable energy sources has set the country back; we may not meet both domestic and military challenges. That is a national tragedy.

Fueling the Future Force stated the following, in powerful language:

"The US Department of Defense (DOD) must prepare now to transition smoothly to a future in which it does not depend on petroleum. This is no small task: up to 77 percent of DOD's massive energy needs—and most aircraft, ground vehicles, ships and weapon systems that DOD is purchasing today—depend on petroleum fuel. Yet, while many of today's weapons and transportation systems are unlikely to change dramatically or be replaced for decades, the petroleum needed to operate DOD assets may *not* remain affordable, or even reliably available, for the lifespan of these systems.

To ready America's armed forces for tomorrow's challenges, DOD should ensure that it can operate all of its systems on non-petroleum fuels by 2040. This thirty-year time frame reflects market indicators pointing toward both higher demand for petroleum and increasing international competition to acquire it. *Moreover, the geology and economics of producing petroleum will ensure that the market grows tight long before petroleum reserves are depleted* [my emphasis].

Some estimates indicate that the current global reserve-to-production (R/P) ratio—how fast the world will produce all currently known recoverable petroleum reserves at the current rate of production—is less than 50 years. Thus, given projected supply and demand, we cannot assume that oil will remain affordable or that supplies will be available to the United States reliably thirty years hence."[3]

Seeing a map of the countries with oil reserves to sell to the highest bidder enabled the authors of *Fueling the Future Force* to present some stark geopolitical realizations:

Ominously, many major suppliers to the United States could produce their current proved reserves in a fairly short time horizon if they continue at the present rate: for example, the R/P ratio for Canada (the top supplier to the United States in 2009, providing more than 20 percent of total oil imports) stands at about 28 years today. For the United States itself, it is 11 years. The only countries with current R/P ratios longer than 75 years are Venezuela, Iran, Iraq, Kuwait and the United Arab Emirates.[4]

As noted above, fracking technology may have added another thirteen years to the US oil supply, but it is a depleting resource.

Almost Half of US Oil Comes from the Persian Gulf and OPEC

The United States imports 138,144 barrels of oil monthly from OPEC countries and the Persian Gulf, according to the US Energy Information Agency. A war between Iran and Israel or the United States would totally disrupt the American oil supply from the Persian Gulf, which flows through the Strait of Hormuz, on the Iranian coast. About 35 percent of the petroleum traded by sea passes through the Strait of Hormuz.

The International Energy Agency *World Energy Outlook* of 2012

This report from the prestigious Paris-based organization correctly predicted that advances in drilling technology would produce an upsurge in North American energy output. It predicted that the United States would overtake Saudi Arabia and Russia to become the planet's leading oil producer by 2020. This is partly true due to a decline in oil production by Saudi Arabia and Russia. At best, the global supply of oil is not going to grow appreciably, while global demand still increases. In the United States, the prediction of the rise of American oil and gas production was met with great jubilation. However, the IEA report noted that "much is riding on Iraq's success. Without this supply growth from Iraq, oil markets would be set for difficult times."[5] We must remember that the United States is still an oil-importing nation, and oil and gasoline prices are set globally, no matter that we produce more oil for domestic consumption or sale.

Burning Fossil Fuels Is Burning the Planet

In 2012, the International Energy Agency reported, "Taking all new developments and policies into account, the world is still failing to put the global energy system onto a more sustainable path." Indeed, this most shocking part of the report was totally ignored by the national media. The IEA determined that even accounting for policy commitments already made or contemplated by world governments, CO_2 emissions are expected to rise precipitously over the next two decades, resulting in a temperature increase of 3.6 degrees C.

We are already seeing what less than 1 degree can do, with Superstorm Sandy and hurricanes Harvey, Irma, Maria, Florence, and Michael. The drastic drought in one-third of the nation, wildfires in the West, Category 5 hurricanes, catastrophic flooding destroying crops in the Midwest, and the rise in sea levels and storm surges are causing great suffering all around the world, not just in the United States. Millions of people have been dislocated to become refugees.

China, India, and All Parts of the World Demand Oil Now

It is not hard to grasp that the American public may not have seen this all coming down the road so quickly. What we have here is a situation where China's demand for oil is almost as high as for the United States; China imported 8.4 million barrels a day in 2017, while the US imported 10.1 million barrels. China is buying one-half of all Iraqi oil, and they accept that country's strict restrictions on profit. This is coupled with a surprisingly quick shortfall in global production, partially due to lack of engineers, fewer drilling platforms, and the lack of easily reachable oil, as we shall see.

In 2016, the price of Brent Crude was $34 per barrel. In 2019, Brent Crude is hovering around $63 per barrel. It has been forecast that the price will stay down until 2025, due to a temporary glut due to sluggish economies in the world. Not enough jobs are being created for the world population. This gives us a very small window to use less expensive oil to rebuild our infrastructure and produce enough solar cell farms, wind farms, biofuel, and LFTRs for around-the-clock electricity. Will we be wise enough to do that?

Jet Fuel Is the Most Difficult to Produce

The Department of Defense report states that 56 percent of military oil demand is for jet fuel. Jet aircraft engines have high energy requirements, which can only be provided by chemical fuels. Electricity does not give airplanes the immediate power boost needed to lift big jets off the runway.

Solar energy derived from biofuels is one hope to fuel jet airplanes, yet scaling up that technology has not yet been achieved. During that endeavor, it will be necessary to scale back the amount of jet fuel that is consumed by Air Force and Navy jets; we must also cut back on the eighty-seven thousand civilian jet flights made each day. The military is rapidly advancing the use of lighter drone aircraft to reduce the amount of jet fuel required to accomplish their missions.

Assuming such a huge consumption level, as the price of oil increases, there will be a massive need for biofuels for jet planes, and there will be fewer affordable flights offered to travelers. But there is hope. As reported on "60 minutes" on June 23, 2019, Marshall Medoff and his chemists have developed an electronic accelerator beam to extract sugar from cellulose which provides a biofuel that can be used to operate cars and aircraft with a 77% lower emission of carbon dioxide. These sugars from cellulose also will provide biodegradable plastic, needed to save our oceans and sea life. The production of this biofuel needs to be scaled up as rapidly as possible. Medoff's company, located in Wakefield, Massachusetts is called Xylecco. Xylecco Corporation needs a wise and forward-looking billionaire or two, to rapidly replace regular plastic with biodegradable plastic. Also, the aviation industry will begin to collapse, due to the fact that oil will be unaffordable and/or unavailable in 20-30 years unless the world has Xylecco's biofuel from cellulose.

Global Competition for Oil Leaves America with Less Available Oil

The wars in Iraq and Afghanistan were fought under the policy of pursuing our national interests, but it did not work out that way. Instead, the Bush administration alienated much of the world against the United States, as witnessed by the huge demonstrations just before our unjustified invasion of Iraq. *Fueling the Future Force* includes a map that delivers a strong visual message: the last remaining oil that is easy to extract is in the hands of nations that are *not* our reliable allies.

The ten-plus years of occupation in Afghanistan has also met fierce resistance by the Pashtun tribes, who are forty-nine million strong and live in Pakistan and Afghanistan. Some Pashtuns have joined the Taliban. The Pashtun and their allies drove the British and the Russians from their homeland. After all, it is their land. The temporary blocking of the Khyber Pass by the Pakistani Pashtun backed up sixty-five hundred American trucks, mostly with oil, for a period of eleven days. This is just one clear example of how people who are unhappy with US policies can totally cut off military oil supply lines. Pakistan protested US drone attacks by blocking NATO and American gasoline supply lines.

The United States is no longer seen as a global peacekeeper or as the world's policeman because of those clear acts of unilateral invasion, dominant military power, and decades of occupations. The Iraq war was a premeditated act of killing, not merely collateral damage. It took over eighty-five thousand Iraqi civilian lives, mostly women and children, as of 2010, and two million civilians were forced out of their homes to become refugees.

Most importantly, the United States has spent so much on these wars, and the total military-industrial complex budget, that it has contributed largely to the $21 trillion national debt. Clearly, bankruptcy from unnecessary military expenditures is not in our national interest.

The Real National Interest Is Producing Electric Cars and Electricity from Solar, Wind, and LFTRs

The endless requests for more military funding is justified by what the politicians call America's national interests. This evasion of reality by the politicians will now come to the foreground of the debate on what constitutes the national interest. After all, the military is not the only group that will be affected by the coming gasoline crunch; the American people who have been forced by suburban sprawl to buy cars and fuel to get to work and earn a living will struggle to survive. Millions of us need to be working at home and moving data around rather than moving bodies around. We also need to build rapid transit systems in the suburbs and new towns across America in order to reduce carbon dioxide, take cars off the road, and decrease the cost of living in the suburbs by owning fewer cars per family.

Table 2
Cost of Gasoline per Gallon in Europe and the United States

(In US dollars per gallon, including taxes)

United States	$2.99
Netherlands	$7.46
Italy	$7.27
UK	$6.57
Germany	$6.43
France	$6.97

Source: Statista, Transportation and Logistics, "Gasoline Prices in Selected Countries Worldwide as of April 16, 2018 (in US Dollars per Gallon)"

The real reason why American gasoline prices are so low is because the federal gas tax has not gone up since 1993. However, Americans pay other taxes to partially cover the cost of driving cars. The Department of Transportation should provide funding to fill the millions of potholes throughout the northern states, where freeze and thaw occurs. The federal budget lacks enough revenue to meet the basic needs of the nation; tax cuts for the rich have diminished the government's ability to serve the actual needs of the nation. Congress needs to address this problem that it has created. The conservative call for small government is really a call to lower taxes on the rich, who fund the re-election campaigns of politicians.

In 2018, gasoline prices were about $3.00 per gallon in the United States. However, this is clearly a short delay, once the current oil glut is consumed. The global appetite for oil has not vanished. This is an excellent time to use less costly oil to build the new solar and wind farms and thorium reactors that we will sorely need in the future.

In April 2011, US gasoline prices were $3.79 per gallon. In a poll by the Associated Press, two-thirds of those questioned said that gas cost spikes would cause serious financial hardship. In December 2018, France proposed to raise gas prices, and protestors hit the streets with violent responses.

The authors of these long-range planning military reports are free to tell the truth. Military planners are not obligated to the financial elite, corporations, the administration, or Congress. In fact, it is their job to plan for the future of the military and to speak truth to the generals and admirals with an open mind.

The Economic Growth Model Based on Oil Is Stalling Out

Jeremy Rifkin has underscored the problem with rising economic growth, based on oil as follows:

"When the price of oil passed the $100 per barrel mark, something unthinkable just a few years earlier, spontaneous protests and riots broke out in twenty-two countries because the steep rise in the price of cereal grains—tortilla protests in Mexico and rice riots in Asia. The fear of widespread political unrest sparked a global discussion around the oil-food connection. With 40% of the human race living on $2 per day or less, even a marginal shift in the price of staples could mean widespread peril. By 2008, the price of soybeans and barley had doubled, wheat had almost tripled, and rice had quintupled.

The United Nations Food and Agriculture Organization (FAO) reported that a record one billion human beings were going to bed hungry. The fear spread as middle class consumers in the developed countries began to be affected by the steep oil price rise. The price of basic items in stores shot up. Gasoline and electricity prices soared. So did the price of construction materials, pharmaceutical products and packaging materials—the list was endless. By late spring, prices were becoming prohibitive and purchasing power began plummeting around the world. In July of 2008, the global economy shut down. That was the great economic earthquake that signaled the beginning of the end of the fossil fuel era."[6]

Each new effort to regain the economic growth of the past decade will stall out at around $150 per barrel. This wild gyration between growth and collapse is the endgame, according to Rifkin:

"While speculators may have added fuel to the fire, the incontrovertible fact is for the past several decades we have been consuming three and a half barrels of oil for every new barrel we find. This reality is what determines our present condition and future prospects."[7]

The Era of Easy Oil Is Nearly Gone; Hard-to-Get Oil Costs Much More

At this writing in September 2018, with US gasoline prices at $2.99 per gallon, it is not too hard to grasp what the future holds in store. The International Energy Agency, which governments rely on for their energy information and forecasts, may have put the issue of global peak oil production to rest in its "2010 World Energy Outlook" report. According to the IEA, global peak production of crude oil probably occurred in 2006 at seventy million barrels per day. The admission stunned the international oil community and sent shudders down the spines of global businesses whose lifeline is crude oil. The International Energy Agency examined the long-term yields of the world's largest producing oil fields, which contain the easy oil that supplies the bulk of the world's energy. The results were stunning: those fields are expected to lose 75 percent of their productive capacity over the next twenty-five years, which will eliminate fifty-two million barrels per day from the oil supplied to the whole world. This means that by 2031, we either find new oil to replace those fifty-two million barrels or shift to less-expensive renewable energy resources.

Michael T. Klare is a professor of peace and world security studies at Hampshire College and published *The Race for What's Left: The Global Scramble for the World's Last Resources.*[8] His article, "A Tough-Oil World," posted on Huffington Post on March 13, 2012, provides a brief but stunning analysis of the huge reserves of hard-to-get oil around the globe. He wrote:

"Those who claim that the Petroleum Age is far from over often point to these reserves as evidence that the world can still draw on immense supplies of untapped fossil fuels. And it is certainly conceivable that, with the application of advanced technologies and a total indifference to environmental consequences, these resources will indeed be harvested. But easy oil it is not."[9]

However, we can no longer ignore the massive and pervasive destructive power of global warming, which has cost $1.5 trillion so far, according to the National Center for Environmental Information. How can anyone be so subservient to money as to not see the oncoming destruction? The chief executive officers of the major oil companies need to do advanced long-range planning and realize that we must all shift to investing in renewable energy now. We will need many years of using oil before we can replace it entirely.

Canada's Tar Sands and the Keystone XL Pipeline

Klare described what tough oil involves as follows:

"Until now, Canada's tar sands have been obtained through a process akin to strip mining, utilizing monster shovels to pry a mixture of sand and bitumen out of the ground. But most of the near-surface bitumen in the tar-sands-rich Alberta has now been exhausted, which means all future extraction will require a far more complex and costly process. Steam will have to be injected into deeper concentrations to melt the bitumen and allow its recovery by massive pumps. This requires a colossal investment of infrastructure and energy, as well as the construction of treatment facilities for all the resulting toxic wastes. According to the Canadian Energy Research Institute, the full development of Alberta's oil sands would require a minimum investment of $218 billion over the next 25 years, not including the cost of building pipelines to the United States (such as the Keystone XL) for processing in U.S. refineries.

Tough oil reserves like these may provide most of the world's new oil in the years ahead. One thing is clear:

even if they can replace easy oil in our lives, the cost of everything oil-related—whether the gas at the pump, in oil-based products, in fertilizers, in just about every nook and cranny of our lives—is going to rise in price. Get used to it. If things proceed as presently planned, we will be in hock to big oil for decades to come."[10]

This is the catastrophe of the century, if we are so weak and blind as to let it happen.

And don't forget the final cost: If all these barrels of oil and oil-like substances are truly produced from the least inviting places on this planet, then for decades to come we will continue to massively burn fossil fuels, creating ever more greenhouse gases as if there were no tomorrow. And here is the sad truth: if we proceed down the tough-oil path instead of investing massively in alternative energies, we may foreclose any hope of averting the most catastrophic consequences of a hotter and more turbulent planet. So, yes there is oil out there. But no, it won't be cheaper, no matter how much there is. And yes, the oil companies can get it, but looked at realistically, who would want it?[11]

Indeed, only those who worship money and do not care about the fate of humanity would want it.

Here is another perspective on why we must take action now: In 2011, Thomas Friedman, a columnist for the *New York Times,* wrote an article titled "Planet Earth is Full." Friedman cited the work of Paul Gilding, an Australian environmentalist-entrepreneur, who described our crisis in his book, *The Great Disruption: Why Climate Change Will Bring on the End of Shopping and the Birth of a New World.* Gilding first mentions the Global Footprint Network, an alliance of scientists, which has concluded that right now, global growth is using about 1.5 earths; we are using up the earth's resources far faster than they can be replenished. We are eating into our future even now. But Gilding is an optimist. As the impact of the Great Disruption hits us, he said, "our response will be proportionally dramatic, mobilizing as we do in war. We will change at a scale and speed we can barely imagine today, completely transforming the economy, including our energy and transport industries, in just a few short decades."[10]

We Need to Give Government Leaders the Courage to Act

The Obama administration was aware of the urgent need to advance a new National Renewable Energy Program to transition from oil to renewable energy sources by 2040 in order to avoid the dire consequences of economic collapse, so he took action with the DOD and the Department of Energy. All the while, most of the Congress was unable to see into the future and determine what it will require. That is why Congress needs to implement a Green New Deal as soon as possible.

When the 1973 oil crisis hit, people took to the streets because they wanted cheap gasoline; they wanted the government to make sure they would have gas to get to work, school, and shopping. We do have the time now, in theory, of three decades to accomplish the daunting tasks ahead; however, delay is not an option.

The elite-controlled media need to make people aware that a global gasoline shortage crisis is steadfastly approaching, and the government must make long-range plans in order to meet the challenge. Today, we are sleepwalking and finding it very difficult to process these realities. The oil-driven economy has made it so easy for Americans to believe that the time for accelerated action can be pushed into the future. Making a sustainable transition from fossil fuels to renewable energies requires a large amount of affordable fossil fuels from which to work and less than a generation of time.

Alex Kuhlman, in his 2006 article "Peak Oil and the Collapse of Commercial Aviation," states the case well:

"Today's market mechanisms are incapable of taking into account the long lead times and resources required to balance supply and demand, and ultimately replace fossil fuels. With oil production declining in almost every nation outside of the Middle East, and spare capacity already quickly disappearing throughout the system, the phenomena of peak oil itself and a pending decline is almost self-evident and hardly needs defending. While the potential apocalyptic implications are far more difficult to digest, they cannot be wished away.

Optimists may argue that technology, the market, brilliant scientists, and comprehensive government programs are going to hold things together. However, with an acute lack of awareness, of time, knowledge, capital, energy, political will, and international collaboration, it is difficult to see how business can continue as usual. A new path must be chosen to conserve the underlying fossil fuel base required to develop and implement sustainable energy sources capable of running even a substantial fraction of countries such as the USA. Otherwise, we may lack the tools to move forward to replace a fluid so cheap, abundant and versatile."[11]

We can conclude from these reports that the production of solar and wind energy, electric cars, biofuels, and thorium nuclear reactors is now a necessity and must be in place over the next thirty years. We are truly challenged to undertake nation building at home as never before. We will need oil to build a new economic platform. However, we are in a global battle, a Third World War, to stop global warming's destruction. We need to mobilize now to stop the death and destruction of global warming and provide energy, livelihoods, and transportation for the nation and the world.

Chapter 4 will show how sun, wind, and thorium reactor power can provide a superabundant amount of energy to increase our material abundance, provided we have the political awareness and will to do the right thing.

Chapter 4

Superabundant Energy Provides Wealth for All

Wind, Solar Power, and Thorium Reactors Produce the Lowest Cost Energy

In 2014, the average residential cost of electricity in the United States was 12 cents per kilowatt-hour. An article in the *New York Times*, "Solar and Wind Energy Start to Win on Price vs. Conventional Fuels," reported that "the cost of providing electricity from wind and solar power has plummeted over the last five years, so much so that in some markets renewable generation is now cheaper than coal or natural gas. For example, in Texas, Austin Energy signed a deal to receive twenty years of electricity from a solar farm for less than five cents per KWH. The article also stated that the Grand River Dam Authority in Oklahoma signed a new agreement with a wind farm expected to be completed in 2014, saying, Grand River estimated the deal would save its customers roughly $50 million from the project."

> According to a study by the investment banking firm Lazard, the cost of utility scale solar energy is as low as 5.6 cents a kilowatt-hour, and wind as low as 1.4 cents. In comparison, natural gas comes in at 6.1 cents a kilowatt-hour on the low end and coal at 6.6 cents. Without subsidies, the firm's analysis shows, solar costs about 7.2 cents a kilowatt-hour at the low end, with wind at 3.7 cents.[1]

We Could Meet All of Our Electricity Needs with Wind Power Alone

In 2012, researchers at Stanford University and the University of Delaware ran a computer model and discovered that wind power alone could meet all of our electricity needs. We can install large concentrations of wind turbines offshore and inland, and they can be spaced so as not to affect each other. "Saturation Wind Power Potential and its Implications for Wind Energy," by Mark Z. Jacobson and Christina L. Archer, was published in the *Proceedings of the National Academy of Sciences*.[2] Their computer model determined that wind farms can be built with no interference between turbines, resulting in the conclusion that we can supply all of the nation's energy needs from wind power alone, if we so choose, although that is not realistic in the short time we have remaining. We also must accelerate the use of solar power, biofuel from cellulose, and safe nuclear energy.

Solar Thermal Electric Power Plants

Solar thermal power, with heat storage to provide electricity 24/7, is one of the leading choices at this time because of its reliability and its smaller use of water, which has become scarce in many regions. Solar thermal power can also be used for desalinization, which has already become necessary to meet water needs in many regions of the world. Make no mistake: the demand for water has already reached shortage levels in ten major US cities and in other places around the world. We need to fund desalinization plants throughout the world.

At this writing, solar thermal power has good prospects, as it generates heat and does not require rare earth metals. Solar thermal uses concentrated solar thermal technology, in which mirrors concentrate sunlight on a boiler to produce heat. The heat is then used to produce steam, which drives highly efficient turbines to generate electricity. Here we are in the twenty-first century, using steam power again. However, the energy to drive that process comes from the sun, not from coal or other fossil fuels, which also came from the sun, but were given to humankind as a precious safety factor until we learned to use the sun's radiation directly for the generation of energy.

In 2009, BrightSource Energy, based in California, has built fourteen solar thermal power plants that will collectively supply more than 2.6 gigawatts of electricity, which is enough to serve about 1.8 million new homes. Another Bright Source project, Ivanpah, is providing a levelized cost of energy of $0.146 per kilowatt-hour.[3] Ivanpah is the largest solar thermal plant in the world, at this writing.

Solar thermal plants are typically built on a large scale. Solar thermal plants have the following advantages: (1) They work best when it is hottest and demand is greatest. (2) The heat can be stored, allowing the electricity to be available at all times. (3) Their turbine generators can be supplemented with hydrogen or biogas boilers to inexpensively add more steam, enabling them to perform as reliably as a fossil-fueled power plant. (4) It dramatically reduces carbon dioxide. (5) Dry-cooling can replace water-cooling using Stirling engines. This is very important in areas where there is a water shortage. (6) Steam generated from solar thermal collectors can help drive the turbines at existing coal and natural gas plants, thus reducing fuel costs and CO_2 emissions, until they can be totally replaced with 100 percent solar thermal, wind power, or hydrogen storage. (7) Steam-driven electric power generation is old, well-known, safe, and reliable for centuries to come. Solar thermal power is the safest option of any other conventional form of energy production such as nuclear, coal, or natural gas. (8) Solar thermal can not only generate electricity but could also extract hydrogen from water. (9) It is cost competitive with traditional energy plants and is by far the most economical and reliable choice when the cost of warming the atmosphere is included in the calculations. With climate change costing billions of dollars in destruction each year, we need to use true cost accounting when assessing energy production.

Hacking Photosynthesis

As described in the book *Abundance*, by Peter Diamandis and Steven Kotler, the Department of Energy is pursuing another pathway to meet our fuel and food needs:

> The Agency is also interested in hacking photosynthesis. Secretary Chu's Sun Shot Initiative has now funded the Joint Center for Artificial Photosynthesis, a $122 million

multi-institution project being led by Caltech, Berkeley and Lawrence Livermore National Laboratory. JCAP's goal is to develop light absorbers, catalysts, molecular linkers, and separation membranes—all the necessary components for faux photosynthesis. "We're designing an artificial photosynthesis process," says Dr. Harry Atwater, director of Caltech Center for Sustainable Energy Research and one of the project's lead scientists. "By 'artificial' I mean there's no living or organic component in the whole system. We're basically turning sunlight, water, and CO_2 into storable, transportable fuels—we call 'solar fuels'—to address the other two-thirds of our energy consumption needs that normal photovoltaics miss."[4]

Not only will these solar fuels be able to power our cars and heat our buildings, Atwater believes that he can increase the efficiency of photosynthesis tenfold, perhaps a hundredfold—meaning solar fuels could completely replace fossil fuels. "We're approaching a critical tipping point," he says. "It is very likely that, in thirty years, people will be saying to each other, 'Goodness gracious, why did we ever set fire to hydrocarbons to create heat and energy?'"[4]

At this writing, in 2018, we are very far away from scaling up artificial photosynthesis to meet our fuel energy and food plant needs for a planet that is adding 350,000 new babies every day. Once again, we appear to be sleepwalking into the future.

There are many companies involved in the research and production of bio-fuels. Exxon has partnered with Craig Venter's company, Synthetic Genomics, to reliably mass-produce bio oils from algae. As reported in the book *Abundance*, Paul Roessler, who heads the project, summarized their work as follows:

In theory, once perfected, we could run this process continuously and just harvest the oil. The cells just keep cranking it out. This way you don't have to harvest all of the cells, instead just scoop up the oils they excrete. Our goal is to get to 10,000 gallons per acre per year, and to get it to work robustly at the level of a two-square-mile facility.

To understand how ambitious Venter's goals are, let's do the math: two square miles is 1,280 acres. At 10,000 gallons of fuel per acre, that's 12.8 million gallons of fuel per year. Using today's average of twenty-five miles per gallon and 12 thousand miles driven per year, two square miles of algae farms produce enough fuel to power around 26,000 cars. So how many acres does it take to power America's entire fleet? With roughly 250 million automobiles in the United States today, that translates to about 18,750 square miles, or about 0.49 percent of the U.S. land area (or about 17 percent of Nevada).[5]

The current goal is for Exxon Mobil to produce ten thousand barrels of algae bio fuel per day, by 2025. The United States imports 10 million barrels of oil per day; we can see how far we have to go to begin to meet our car fuel needs.

Scaling up bio fuels just to meet transportation needs is clearly a huge task. Perhaps we should consider using biofuels for aircraft and use thorium nuclear reactors to produce electricity to recharge car batteries.

A University of Texas at Arlington materials science and engineering team has developed a new photo-electrochemical energy cell that can efficiently store solar energy and deliver electric power twenty-four hours a day, according to KurzweilAI/Accelerating Intelligence.News (July 3, 2015). The article, "A Solar-Energy Storage Cell that Works at Night," states, "It can also be scaled up to provide large amounts of energy, limited only by the size of its chemical storage tanks, according to Fuqiang Liu, an assistant professor in the Materials Science and Engineering Department who led the team. The team is now working on a larger prototype."[6]

China is the largest producer of solar energy; their leaders know they must develop more renewable energy because burning coal has caused so much pollution in large cities that people have to wear masks outside in order to breathe. Now that solar and wind are cheaper than coal and natural gas, global economic systems will pursue the lowest cost energies, according to the most ancient rule of economics: "buy at the lowest cost."

The emergence of low-cost, reliable, renewable, and non-destructive energy will give humankind enough wealth to be distributed to all, providing we design the economic system to that purpose. We do not need a Robin Hood scenario where we take from the rich to give to the poor. What we can have is an original distribution of wealth to all, not redistribution. Those who have abundant wealth now are strongly encouraged to join the Bill Gates and Warren Buffet Giving Pledge to drive the development of regional worker-owner cooperatives as one of their top priorities. In order to save humanity from climate destruction, we need the billionaire class to strongly support the construction of non-carbon-energy-producing plants and electric automobiles.

The World's Largest Investors, with $22.5 Trillion, Call for Climate Change Action

In Singapore, November 20, 2012, Reuters reported, "A coalition of the world's largest investors called on governments to ramp up action on climate change and boost clean-energy investment or risk trillions of dollars in investment disruption of the economy.

In an open letter, the alliance of institutional investors, responsible for managing $22.5 trillion in assets, said rising greenhouse gas emissions and more extreme weather were increasing investment risks globally. The group called for dialogue between investors and government to overhaul climate and energy policies. Current policies are insufficient to avert serious and dangerous impacts from climate change, said the group of investors from the United States, Europe, Asia, and Australia."[7]

The World Bank said that current climate policies meant that the world was heading for a warming of 4 degrees C by 2100. That would trigger deadly heat waves and droughts, cut food supplies, and drive up sea levels, which would flood most coastal areas, as was demonstrated by Superstorm Sandy in New York and New Jersey, which cost $60 billion.

The Creation of Worker-Owner New Towns and Energy Farms with Regional Planning

In order to create work for all, we need to undertake long-range planning for the creation of millions of sustainable jobs. Because energy sources for solar and wind vary in different regions of the United States, we will need to plan for job creation on a regional basis. For example, the Southwest gets enough sunlight to build solar thermal energy plants.

The Southeast and Florida have an abundance of sun radiation and can best use solar thermal, photovoltaics, and wind power. The Northeast, which is very highly populated, with less sun radiation, can import solar and wind power energy from the Plains and the Southeast and even the Southwest.

This can be done with direct current transmission lines, which can transport electricity as far as twenty-four hundred miles with only a 15 percent loss in energy, as estimated in Desertec, a North Africa project which was designed to supply solar electricity to Europe.[8] Thorium nuclear reactors can be used in all regions of the United States for the production of around-the-clock electricity, when the sun doesn't shine and the wind does not blow. These safe mini-reactors can provide electricity to the rural areas and to major cities as well.

Starting with energy supply, regional planning can then move on to build manufacturing facilities and organizations to supply all the basic needs of humankind: food, water, housing, clothing, and most of the goods that are found in department stores, supermarkets, and malls. Regional cooperatives can have contracts with other cooperatives outside of their region, such as seafood cooperatives. Not all of a region's products have to be made within the region. Regional cooperatives can export as much as 25 percent of their products in order to purchase luxury items they cannot or don't want to produce.

For a much more detailed examination of how the Mondragon Cooperative Corporation functions, please see Roy Morrison's excellent first-hand report in his book, *We Build the Road as We Travel*.[9] MCC has developed a new business model and a new banking model that can be replicated around the world to better serve humankind. While MCC has not promoted its model as a path for the future for all, the author has taken the liberty to do so. The MCC model clearly shows a superior economic structure based on the higher values of truth, goodness, justice, and pursuit of the common good; we treasure these values and want to incorporate them in our lives and in the economic system. We cannot have a happy civilization until we do that.

A New Workplace Platform to Replace the Old Platform

Pope Francis has written that the free market system "has been deified";[10] that is, it has claimed to have a god like power, with market forces deciding all economic decisions, based on profit-making and the survival of the fittest. Clearly, the current system cannot be maintained because its so-called godlike powers cannot create enough livelihoods for humanity, nor is it possible to distribute income equitably from the generation of our newly developed wealth. We need a new workplace platform to replace the old platform, which is rapidly sinking into oblivion. However, we cannot make the step from the sinking platform until we establish the new platform, starting with well-planned regional models. Once people can see the true value of the new workplace platform, they can make the transition.

The following chapter will show how to create millions of livelihoods by using conscious planning, design, and implementation.

Chapter 5
How to Create Millions of New Livelihoods

We are challenged now and into the future to be creative in developing new, sustainable jobs for all members of society. We take courage from the fact that the conscious creation of jobs has never been tried before in America; it's an entirely new endeavor. The current market system only creates jobs when people buy a product or a service. Jobs are also created from start-up businesses, of course; however, many of them fail in the first five years for two major reasons: bad business decisions and lack of bank funding when needed to survive or thrive.

The Mondragon banking model takes care of the first problem by replacing the general manager and shifting him to another cooperative job. The Mondragon Bank tracks the ongoing operations of a new cooperative, and if it starts to have problems and needs funding, the bank will consider the purpose and proceed to authorize funding. If the cooperative needs a new product or service, the bank can help with that also. Millions of jobs can be created or preserved by intelligent and caring banking that is not merely pursuing the profit motive while being unwilling to create enough jobs. In a society of abundance, based on cheap and nearly inexhaustible energy, good cooperative banking will have far fewer risks.

We will need to create millions of jobs for people who work with their hands and muscles. Millions of jobs will be created by building new towns of the twenty-first century. Millions of construction jobs will be created to replace the nation's infrastructure of bridges, roads, railroads, and so on. We will need to build a new electric grid to accommodate superabundant solar, wind, and safe nuclear power production. We will need to plant billions of trees globally, as this is the fastest way to absorb carbon dioxide and dramatically slow down global warming.

In Order to Stop Global Warming, We Need to Manufacture Massive Numbers of Electric Cars

While new towns for the twenty-first century will have well-designed rapid transit systems, we will still need to build millions of electric cars for suburban commuters and for interstate travel. In 2017, Americans bought 17.3 million automobiles, and 199,826 were electric.[1] We will also need to build enough renewable energy facilities to provide electricity for those millions of electric cars that we will produce each year.

We Need to Build Rapid Transit Systems for the Sprawling Suburbs and Reduce the Number of Gas-Guzzlers on the Roads by 66 Percent

We can reduce the number of family cars needed to just one, when we build new towns with excellent transit systems that take us to work, shopping, schools, churches, exercise, and so on. We also need to develop a transportation plan for the suburbs with rapid transit buses and ten-seat vans to deliver people to work, shopping, and recreation.

While we can reduce the number of cars needed per family by 66 percent, however, population growth will continue to need a large number of buses, automobiles, and trucks.

We have built suburbs and interstate highways across the land, so it makes sense to produce new cars to use them. We have a huge task before us that will require many engineers from the military contractors, and it will require all automobile manufacturers to gradually produce millions of electric cars. We are way behind the supply needed. Time is of the essence.

Chapter 7 will show how to create millions of jobs in the housing and housing-related industries, which drive 25 percent of the economic system.

Sustainable Agriculture

Sustainable agriculture is the production of food, fiber, or other plant or animal products using farming techniques that replenish the top soil without petroleum-based fertilizers. The techniques used will protect the environment and public health, create vibrant communities, and promote animal welfare. Sustainable agriculture produces healthful food without keeping future generations from doing the same. This means, of course, the gradual dismantling of the current industrialized agriculture system. We will need to ban the use of Round Up and many other chemicals that get in our ground water and cause widespread cancer.

Factory farming of animals could be entirely eliminated. Animals could be given free range and care. There would be no more confining animals so they cannot turn around in their cages. Antibiotics and drugs for quick growth would no longer be used, as animals would grow at their own natural rate. The use of antibiotics needs to be phased out. We can eliminate millions of health problems, including cancer, from using pesticides. By using responsible management of livestock waste, sustainable farming will also protect humans from exposure to pathogens, toxins, and other hazardous pollutants that run off into lakes and rivers.

Methane produced by cattle is the second-largest emitter of global warming pollution. We need to eat more seafood, chicken, turkey, and quail. Fresh quail (not frozen) is the best meat I have ever eaten, bar none.

When fully implemented, sustainable farming and careful food processing could employ 15 percent of the working population. In this manner, the nation would enjoy their food, free from the callbacks of contaminated products by those who would use dangerous techniques for productivity increases and more profit. We could begin to reduce cancer rates by the millions, simply by redesigning the agricultural/animal production systems.

Regional planners would identify arable areas and set aside farmland to be conserved for current and future generations. It has been reported that 70 percent of the top soil has vanished due to industrialized farming techniques. The solution is well known. Sustainable farmers plant winter crops that can be turned into the soil. Then, they do not till the soil, but plant seeds directly into the newly enriched soil. By using these techniques, the top soil is *not* turned into dust that is blown away by the wind. Also, Iowa farmers have reported massive loss of topsoil when too much rainfall wipes out their crops and then washes away topsoil from plowed fields.

Sustainable agriculture is a classic example of adopting new methods that are not driven by greed and the pursuit of more and more profits. It is far more important to create millions of living-wage jobs for people who work with their hands, who cannot find jobs in the high-tech economic structure or in professional jobs that require a college education. We need to plant millions of trees, globally, as on balance, plants release more oxygen and absorb more carbon dioxide. We need to plant billions of trees to be used in housing construction. We can also trim trees and use the cellulose to provide biofuel, as described above.

Forest management can be given a policy mandate to plant two trees for every tree that is cut down. The use of laminated wood beams is now growing in use in order to replace concrete and steel, which release more carbon dioxide in their production process.

When we employ more people in agriculture, as outlined above, the cost of producing healthy food will increase. This can be offset by government funding that is not wasted on arms production for sale and other military expenditures.

Build Vertically With Low-Rise Construction to Conserve Farmland

When we build new towns, we should build low-rises for residential as well as commercial and institutional buildings, in order to preserve farmland. It is proposed that low-rise buildings be connected to each other by bridges that can provide glass-enclosed spaces for playgrounds, open-air parks, gardens, and places to have outdoor parties. These features would make low-rise living much more enjoyable and sociable. We can construct buildings twelve stories high with laminated wood beams, as is happening in Portland, Oregon.

The Abundance of Wealth and Growth Comes from Harnessed Energy

For those who doubt that the unbridled advances from the use of solar, thorium reactors, and wind power will bring about huge gains in distributed wealth, we can refer to the prescient prescription of Buckminster Fuller, who wrote the following in his prophetic book, *Operating Manual for the Spaceship Earth:*[2]

> "I must observe also that we are not going to sustain life
> at all except by our successful impoundment of more

of the sun's radiant energy aboard our spaceship than we are losing from Earth in the energies of radiation or outwardly rocketed physical matter.

The production of heretofore nonexistent production tools and industrial networks of harnessed energy to do more work that does not cost anything but human time, which is refunded in time gained minutes after the inanimate machinery goes to work. Nothing is spent. Potential wealth has become real wealth. Under lethal emergencies (such as war), vast new magnitudes of wealth come mysteriously into effective operation. We don't seem to be able to afford to do peacefully the logical things we say we ought to be doing to forestall warring— by producing enough to satisfy all world needs.

Being vital, the problems are evolutionary, inexorable, and ultimately unavoidable by humanity. The constantly put-off or under-met costs and society's official bumbling of them clearly prove that man does not know at present what wealth is nor how much of whatever it may be is progressively available to him."[3]

A New Definition of Wealth

Fuller also wrote, "Wealth is the product of the progressive mastery of matter by mind, and is specifically accountable in man-days ... which advance the forward days of humankind.... Because our wealth is continually multiplying in vast degree unbeknownst and unacknowledged formally by human society, our economic accounting systems are unrealistically identifying wealth only as matter and are entering know-how on the books only as salary liabilities; therefore all that we are discovering mutually here regarding the true nature of wealth comes as a complete surprise to world society—to both communism and to capitalism alike. Both social cooperation and individual enterprise interact to produce increasing wealth, all unrecognized by ignorantly assumed lethally competitive systems."

Fuller identifies the true components that produce wealth as intellectual know-how and abundant physical energy combined in a system which is cooperative rather than lethally competitive. He wrote, "Sum totally, we find that the physical component of wealth—energy—cannot decrease and that the metaphysical constituent—know-how—can only increase. This is to say that every time we use our wealth it increases."

For proof that we have thus far unknowingly advanced the forward days of humanity, Fuller offers the following:

> "As a consequence of true wealth's unaccounted, inexorably synergistic multiplication of ever-increasing numbers of humanity's ever-increasing forward days, in this century alone [the twentieth] we have gone from less than 1 percent of humanity being able to survive in any important kind of health and comfort to 44 percent of humanity surviving at a standard of living unexperienced or undreamed before.... It also happened only as a consequence of man's inadvertently becoming equipped synergistically to do progressively more with less." [5]

Clearly, God has endowed humankind with a metaphysical intellect that is the main driving force for our survival, which is now being revealed in advances in renewable energy, technology, computers, information systems, and long-range planning. What is now missing in our human evolutionary advance is the worker-owner cooperative economic structure that equitably distributes the wealth we all create. It is our human values that must guide our intellects, which direct our corporations and governments to create a new social consciousness that will embrace spiritual abundance as well as material abundance.

So now, thanks to the community of worker-owners at Mondragon Cooperative Corporation, we have a new business model and a new banking model. They have eliminated the ignorant conflict between capital and labor by being owners as well as workers. They have established their guiding values based on Catholic social teaching, which includes justice, defined as "giving a person his or her due." They have established a system of democracy at the workplace and set up a distribution of labor wealth profits to all, with upper limits on the amount of money distributed to top management, thereby eliminating greed and the temptation to corruption that is so prevalent in the current unenlightened economic system. In Mondragon, they have taken control of their lives and their community in a marvelous cooperative manner. We need to look through the prism of sharing and cooperation instead of the mirror of egoistic greed and competition.

We Can Have a Four-Day Workweek

With the cooperative business model, we can distribute the abundant wealth created by humankind to all humankind. Increases in productivity, through information technology and robots, can now be distributed back to worker-owners in the form of more leisure time, as well as increased income.

While working with a living wage, people can have a four-day workweek, thus freeing time for other activities, such as the arts and sports. If people want to be more appreciated for their talents, they can achieve that through awards and honors. If others prefer to have more luxuries, they can work part time to earn more money. A four-day workweek will go far in providing enough livelihoods for all, while making room for all to be employed and give everyone the dignity of work.

Worker-Owned Cooperatives Are Not for Everyone

The professions, such as doctors, dentists, attorneys, health care professionals, and others that require extensive college education, would benefit in much the same way as they are today. Those who want to pursue the path of becoming fabulously rich can still do so. We just need another economic structure to provide "a safe place for humanity," as economist Kate Raworth stated in her excellent book, *Doughnut Economics: 7 Ways to Think Like a 21st Century Economist*.[6]

Jobs Need to Be Created for Blacks, Hispanics, Whites: All of Us

We must consciously plan to provide livelihoods for all, especially for those who work with their hands and muscles, such as unskilled laborers, farmers, tree planters and tradesmen. As described above, we can employ millions of people in agriculture, by replacing industrialized farming with sustainable, healthy agriculture. We can also employ millions of workers in construction and we can stabilize housing-related industries. According to the Harvard Joint Center on Housing Studies, housing and related industries drive 25 percent of the economy, which amounts to thirty-nine million jobs in the United States (see chapter 7). We also need to create jobs in forestry to plant millions of trees and other plants to draw down CO_2 and increase biofuel production. Scientists have hacked photosynthesis. Now, we need to scale up the massive production of 15 percent larger plants from that method.

Shifting Money from the Military to Nation Building at Home: The Nation Builder's Industrial Complex

The stage is set, then, for the federal government and the private sector to lead the nation to start building solar farms, wind farms, solar/hydrogen fuel cell kits for homes and offices, safe nuclear power plants, electric cars, and new towns with rapid transit systems, while also providing rapid transit for the suburbs. This will require a smart electrical grid to enable everyone to plug in. A national grid needs to be designed that's not subject to malicious cyberattacks. There is now a demand path for many of the military-industrial complex corporations and their employees to make the rapid shift to develop a nation builder's industrial complex.

There will certainly still be a need for defending the nation from terrorist attacks and cyberattacks. However, the vast majority of military spending has been based on existing and future land wars on foreign soil against sovereign nations. The United States has 268 military installations in Germany and a total of eight hundred bases spread around the world. Approximately 450,000 US servicemen and servicewomen are currently deployed in more than 150 countries. The United States cannot be invaded on land, except through Canada and Mexico. America is protected by the Pacific and the Atlantic from the east and the west, which is strongly guarded by the Air Force, the Navy, and the Coast Guard. We have a missile defense system and a strong military defense, undeniably.

Abraham Lincoln said, "America will never be destroyed from the outside. If we falter and lose our freedoms, it will be because we destroyed ourselves."

The Cold War has been long over. The vast majority of these military bases are in place based on the premise that the projection of military power serves the advancement of international corporations of America and the outsourcing of American manufacturing. Most of this manufacturing needs to be returned home. Outsourcing manufacturing has proven to be a great mistake in terms of the need for nation building at home, which is, today, the real national defense of American families. Families and individuals are paying 53 cents of every tax dollar that supports the counterproductive military-industrial complex. Defense of the homeland is necessary, but invading foreign countries is now considered a huge mistake. Diplomacy is superior to unilateral aggression.

Defense Secretary Gates Blasted the Wars in Iraq and Afghanistan

The former secretary of defense, Robert Gates, bluntly told an audience of West Point cadets, "Any future defense secretary who advises the president to again send a big American land army into Asia or into the Middle East or Africa should have his head examined."[7]

Gates has blasted wars like Iraq and Afghanistan as serious mistakes. In what was his farewell speech before retiring, he set the stage for a major withdrawal of American forces from these two unsustainable wars, which President Obama has largely accomplished. Fighting terrorism is now mostly a job for intelligence and for small, elite strike forces to deal with, including the use of drones.

This can lead to a substantial decrease in military spending as the troops come home, and many of the 950 military bases around the world can be phased out. The stage is set to transfer Pentagon dollars to alternative energy and infrastructure building at home. As we close bases and bring the troops home, we can provide good-paying jobs for them in the nation builder's industrial complex, by building new towns for the twenty-first century. The global economic crisis has demonstrated that an economy based solely on artificial financial wealth, moved around in financial markets, rather than invested in home-grown manufacturing and livelihoods at home, does not create enough good-paying livelihoods to support a large and growing middle class, which is essential to any good economic system. Greed is not good; it is totally destructive to our well-being.

It is a necessity that American international corporations return home and be based here as worker-owned cooperatives, making things and creating sustainable livelihood systems at home and with a corporation structure where workers are seated on the boards of directors in private corporations.

The Government Needs to Shift Resources from Warring to the Domestic Economy

US taxpayers cannot afford to maintain military forces at current levels for four major reasons: (1) We are becoming a debtor country, largely due to the seemingly endless wars and plans for more wars driven by the entrenched profiteering of the military-industrial complex. (2) We cannot afford to spend billions of dollars on oil to maintain a vast military establishment. (3) Social Security and Medicare are very popular earned benefits; Americans must have a minimum of personal financial security and basic health service, and they certainly will not be cut deeply enough to reduce the national deficit while maintaining an enormous national security budget of $1.2 trillion per year (see details below). (4) Over the next three decades, the transition from petroleum to solar, wind, and biofuels will require a total national commitment, both public and private, of trillions of dollars to be invested and paid back.

The top priority of the nation now is to avoid economic collapse and the destruction of the planet, our only home. It is now starkly clear that millions of Americans must shift out of the MIC and have nonmilitary jobs to build a totally new energy and transportation system, using alternative energy to get to their jobs. America's real national interests in defending the nation are the shift from unproductive military ventures and the arms trade to providing renewable energy and good sustainable jobs at home.

The Real National Security Budget Is $1.2 Trillion per Year

America has debt largely because of runaway national security spending and the banking disasters of 2008. The real national security budget is far more than the $700 billion for the Pentagon budget and the supplementary funds for our conflicts in Iraq and Afghanistan. According to a detailed accounting by Christopher Hellman with the Center for Arms Control and Non-Proliferation, the total national security budget is $1.2 trillion a year.[8] Here is the breakdown listed by Hellman: $700 billion for the Pentagon, $40 billion for the intelligence agencies, $71.6 billion for Homeland Security, $129 billion for veterans programs to care for them after they return from the wars, $18 billion for foreign affairs and counterterrorism budgets, $48.5 billion for military and Defense Department retirees, *and $185 billion in interest payments on borrowing related to past Pentagon spending.* All of this totals over $1.2 trillion per year. Throwing money at the military is clearly an unsustainable expenditure, and a few members of Congress are just starting to embrace that fact. The Defense Department has not been fully audited for years by the Congressional Budget Office, and the Pentagon cannot account for $22 billion, and more, in past spending. Clearly, this all has to change.

Shifting Destructive Arms Production to Constructive Energy Projects

The production of arms, military jets, gunships, and tanks is a global sales industry, with the United States providing up to 85 percent (depending on the year) of the global production of lethal weaponry, which can only be used for the destruction of people, homes, military facilities and equipment, infrastructure, buildings, and productive resources all around the world. The United States had $85.3 billion in arms sales in 2011, according to the non-partisan Congressional Research Service. Most sales went to the Gulf region, the most unstable, violent part of the world. This leads to the question, "Is the military-industrial complex setting up the next land war in the Middle East?" Perhaps in Iran?

Strategically, the MIC has placed production plants and warehouses in every state, so members of Congress vote to maintain the jobs that are producing these destructive arms. However, now the military knows that many of these aircraft and vehicles cannot even be used without new renewable fuel sources. They will simply not have enough affordable petroleum supplies by 2040. Future large-scale land wars are wisely opposed by the former secretary of defense; many of these aircraft and vehicles were designed to serve large-scale land wars.

The Pentagon has told Congress that they no longer wanted the C-17; however, enough members of Congress voted to keep these unwanted weapons of destruction in production, in order to keep jobs in their state.

This is how billions of our taxpayer dollars are wasted each year. Those days should be clearly over.

Constructive Work for the MIC Is Now a National Emergency Priority

Congress obviously needs to provide the MIC employees and returning troops with more constructive employment that actually serves the nation. The problem has been that the production of weapons results in such a large profit and such large salaries that it is difficult to shift weapons production to peacetime jobs and profits. In order to make this shift, it will be necessary to undertake projects on a large scale that will benefit the nation and provide employment for the former MIC employees with good salaries. As it turns out, our national emergency needs fit these requirements: we need a totally new energy system, electric grid, transportation systems, affordable housing and infrastructure. We also need to fund basic and applied scientific research at a higher level, which will advance the forward days of humankind far more than warring.

Military Spending Is the Weakest Job Creator

An independent analysis by Robert Polin and Heidi Garret-Peltier at the University of Massachusetts concluded that military spending was the weakest job creator compared with creating jobs in clean energy, health care, and education, or simply returning the money to the private economy in the form of tax cuts.[7]

The Transformation of Consciousness about War

At the close of the twentieth century, Richard J. Barnet wrote a powerful article for the *New Yorker* titled "Reflections after the Cold War." Barnet was the founder of the Institute for Policy Studies and made his transition to the afterlife in 2009. What follows are excerpts from that article, which are relevant today. Barnet wrote:

> "Since the early years of the century, a long process of rethinking has been underway about the uses of military power to advance national political and economic

interests. Gorbachev's "new thinking" is grounded in some of the obvious lessons of the twentieth century. The First World War nearly obliterated the distinction between victors and vanquished; Britain and France suffered such grievous casualties and economic costs that they could sustain neither their empires nor stable economies and robust democracies at home. The Second World War made it clear that high-technology "conventional warfare," however noble the cause, could not be repeated without reducing whole continents to rubble. It was immediately apparent that the atomic bomb was not a weapon in the strict sense, because it could be effectively used by *not* using it. Today, there is a growing consensus that a large-scale nuclear war would destroy all that was to be defended."[10]

The next chapter will show how Pope Francis, Muslim leaders, and the United Nations are sharing a common vision in order to advance material and spiritual abundance in the world.

Chapter 6
The Advancement of Social Consciousness

Social consciousness is seeing together, being aware of the problems and solutions that communities face on a daily basis. It is understanding the oneness, that all things and human beings are interconnected and share the same existence. It is understanding that we are not separate beings, but rather, we are part of the environment and part of each other. Social consciousness is the realization that living in a community which cares about other people is worth sacrificing for. It is the universal recognition of the Golden Rule: "Do unto others as you would have them do unto you." It is also responding to the teachings of Christ, who said, "Love one another. As I have loved you, so should you also love one another" (John 13:34). The more we dialogue together, the more we see things together in the same way or begin to understand the other person's perspective.

The United Nations has been working with a Sustainable Development Solutions Network of thousands of people and organizations. On May 16, 2015, the UN published "The Global Sustainable Development Report," which features a detailed description of proposed indicators and a monitoring framework to launch a data revolution for seventeen sustainable development goals, as follows:[1]

- Goal 1: End poverty in all its forms everywhere.
- Goal 2: End hunger, achieve food security and improved nutrition, and promote sustainable agriculture.
- Goal 3: Ensure healthy lives and promote well-being for all ages.
- Goal 4: Ensure inclusive and equitable quality education and promote life-long learning opportunities for all.

- Goal 5: Achieve gender equality and empower all women and girls.
- Goal 6: Ensure availability and sustainable management of water and sanitation for all.
- Goal 7: Ensure access to affordable, reliable, sustainable, and modern energy for all.
- Goal 8: Promote sustained, inclusive, and sustainable economic growth, full and productive employment, and decent work for all.
- Goal 9: Build resilient infrastructure, promote inclusive and sustainable industrialization, and foster innovation.
- Goal 10: Reduce inequality within and among countries.
- Goal 11: Make cities and human settlements inclusive, safe, resilient, and sustainable.
- Goal 12: Ensure sustainable consumption and production patterns.
- Goal 13: Take urgent action to combat climate change and its impacts.
- Goal 14: Conserve the oceans, seas, and marine resources and only use them for sustainable development.
- Goal 15: Protect, restore, and promote sustainable use of terrestrial ecosystems, sustainably manage forests, combat desertification, reverse land degradation, and halt biodiversity loss.
- Goal 16: Promote peaceful and inclusive societies for sustainable development, provide access for justice for all, and build effective, accountable, and inclusive institutions at all levels.
- Goal 17: Strengthen the means of implementation, and revitalize the global partnership for sustainable development.

These goals, common to all nations, represent an increase in social consciousness based on universal human values. In order to achieve these wonderful global goals, it is clear that we will have to implement a new business model and a new banking model. Unfettered capitalism is a selfish blockade against implementing these goals, while the Mondragon Cooperative Corporation model offers a far better system for implementing the UN's sustainable development goals.

Ruthless competition and the pursuit of making money only (as the primary value) has brought civilization this far and our intellectual know-how has advanced the quality of life for millions. However, we have arrived at a new level of social consciousness and an intense desire to overcome inequality in order to address our major threatening problems, which are destructive climate change, replacing oil, and the need for a sustainable job creation system. Just when it is needed the most, the United Nations has stepped up to unite us and show how we must work together and see together in order to survive and advance as a species.

We propose that all of the nations of the world need to build a regional economic model based on the Mondragon prototype. The countries of Europe and the Middle East, especially Iran, Saudi Arabia, and Egypt, need to demonstrate the benefits of this model to give hope to their people. Likewise, the countries of Asia, such as Japan, China, and North Korea, need to demonstrate the Mondragon regional economic model to benefit their millions of people. If anyone has a better economic model to serve humankind, now is the time to bring it forth.

The UN, Pope Francis, and Muslim Clergy Lead the World to Stop Greenhouse Gas Emissions

There are 193 nations in the UN General Assembly. There are 2.18 billion Christians in the world and 1.6 billion Muslims, which totals 3.78 billion, or over half of the world population, whose leaders have joined to save the earth from further destruction from burning fossil fuels.

The *Washington Post* published an article on August 18, 2015, titled "Muslim Leaders Support Islamic Declaration on Climate Change." It reported, "Muslim leaders and scholars from 20 countries made a joint declaration Tuesday [August 18, 2015] at a conference in Istanbul, calling all nations worldwide to address climate change. The statement also quotes Islamic texts, suggesting a religious imperative to care for the environment and calling on the world's 1.5 billion Muslims to play an active role in these efforts."

The United Nations Sustainable Development Goals are joined by Pope Francis's *Encyclical on Climate Change and Inequality—On Care for Our Common Home.*

Pope Francis wrote:

> When we speak of the "environment," what we really mean
> is a relationship existing between nature and the society

which lives in it. Nature cannot be regarded as something separate from ourselves or as a mere setting in which we live. We are part of nature, included in it and thus in constant interaction with it. Recognizing why a given area is polluted requires a study of the workings of society, its economy, its behavior patterns, and the ways it grasps reality. Given the scale of change, it is no longer possible to find a specific, discrete answer for each part of the problem. It is essential to seek comprehensive solutions which consider the interactions within natural systems themselves and with social systems. We are faced not with two separate crises, one environmental and one social, but rather with one complex crisis which is both social and environmental. Strategies for a solution demand an integrated approach to combating poverty, restoring dignity to the excluded, and at the same time protecting nature.[2]

In a concise and brilliant introduction to Pope Francis's encyclical, Naomi Oreskes writes:

While the word "capitalism" does not appear in the letter, the word "market" (or its variants) appears nineteen times, usually in a critical context. The pope is not advocating communism, but he is asking us to acknowledge that we live in a world where the ideology of the market place is so dominant that most of us can scarcely imagine an alternative, and where those who try are dismissed as unrealistic, irrational, naïve, faint-hearted, sentimental, romantic, out of step, or (if in America) communists. He is asking us to examine the creed of "individualism, unlimited progress, competition, consumerism, the unregulated market."[3]

Here we see the workings of the selfish ego. The ego loves individualism and division, keeping us separate from each other, competing with each other for selfish gain, rather than joining together for the common good of all. The ego therefore generates divisions, conflicts, polarization, anger, and distrust.

When what we need is to work together in cooperation for our common good and our individual good, which is balanced and beneficial to the individual and to society as a whole. It is *seeing together* through the prism of cooperation and sharing, rather than seeing through the prism of competition for selfish gain and power over others. Again, we see how the ego creates the false self and tries to evade our transformation to the true self, as described more clearly in the works of Richard Rohr, Thomas Merton, Albert Nolan and others.

Richard Rohr, the spiritual translator, wrote this about the true self:

> "What's happening in prayer is that you're presenting yourself for the ultimate gaze, the ultimate mirroring, the gaze of God. Little by little you become more naked before the perfectly accepting gaze. It's like love making. You slowly disrobe and become mirrored perfectly in the gaze of God. You gradually allow yourself to be seen, to be known in every nook and cranny, nothing hidden, nothing denied, nothing disguised. And the wonderful thing is, after a while you feel so safe and you don't have to pretend anymore. You recognize your need for mercy, your own utter inadequacy and littleness, that the best things you've ever done have been for mixed and false motives. And the worst things you have ever done were done because you were *unconscious*.
>
> "Someone is giving their self to me! Someone is sustaining me," you feel like shouting. Now this experience of being sustained, being given to without any just cause, knowing that you didn't earn it, causes the whole worthiness game to break apart. The true self experiences reality as radical grace. Who is worthy? No one is worthy. The true self knows this and lives quietly, calmly and contentedly inside of its radical unworthiness. You can do this because you ironically know that you are totally worthy, but it has nothing to do with you! Your

worthiness is entirely given to you (Ephesians 2:3-4). All true holiness is reflected glory."

Julian of Norwich and Thomas Merton have both said that what is happening in prayer is that you are allowing God to recognize God's self in you and that's what God always loves and cannot *not love*. That is God's new and everlasting covenant with humanity (Jeremiah 31, 33:19-20), promised by the prophets and ritualized in the Eucharist. The human problem is solved from the beginning, and at its core."[4]

Prayer, then, is how we overcome the selfish ego, by drawing closer and closer in our conversation with God. And by doing so, we learn how to sidestep and transcend the ego and refocus on good things, such as loving and being loved. Julian of Norwich also said, "All is well, and all will be well." This is a mystic saying, meaning, "God's got you and everything covered, so sleep well."

The next chapter will demonstrate how young people can afford to buy a home earlier in life and how the housing-related industries can avoid boom-and-bust cycles and be stabilized, while creating millions of sustainable jobs, building affordable workforce housing. However, success requires some changes in the economic system: we must make education free, so that graduates are not burdened with over $100,000 of tuition debt; we must raise the contribution of the private sector to 401(k) accounts from a paltry 3.0 percent of salary to 7.5 percent. This is just economic common sense in order to enable young people to be able to buy a home and have a good family life.

Chapter 7

The Home Ownership Plan (HOP): How to Enable Young People to Buy a Home and Stabilize the Housing-Related Industries

Housing is the costliest item in the family budget, which means that people must save large sums of money for a large down payment in order to secure the loan. Young people need assistance early in their working lives to be able to save enough to buy a home. This can be done through the Home Ownership Plan, which features a tax-free savings account, similar to a 401(k). Canada already has a similar plan.

Legislation for the Home Ownership Plan was co-drafted by Representative Robert Wexler, under the title, "Restore the American Dream Act," HR 3557.[1] After Wexler resigned from Congress, the legislation was adopted by his successor, Representative Ted Deutch (D-Florida).

Disclaimer

This bill was drafted before college costs increased so much that students are graduating with crushing debts of $100,000 or more. Once this debt burden is eliminated by free college tuition, the Home Ownership Plan will be of great benefit as described below. It will also be necessary to raise the employer contribution to 401(k) plans to 7.5 percent of gross salary, as in other countries. Finally, almost 80 percent of workers in the United States are working from paycheck to paycheck and need more income to buy a home.

Robert Reich, the former secretary of the Department of Labor, described the reasons for this in his article, "Almost 80% of U.S. Workers Live from Paycheck to Paycheck. Here's Why."[2]

The reason is that labor unions have not been strongly adopted by the general public. Therefore, they have no voice in the decisions of large corporations. These are the three major reasons that a whole generation of young people are being shut out from buying a home and a way of building wealth. Also, the median contribution by private sector corporations in America to 401(k)s is a disgracefully low 3 percent, while it needs to be 7.5 percent to enable a person to use the Home Ownership Plan to buy a home early in life and have enough for retirement.

How the Home Ownership Plan Works

The Home Ownership Plan is (HOP) only for first-time homebuyers. Here is how it works: when young people first enter the workplace, the employer can give them the choice of enrolling in the HOP or in the company's retirement plan. A key feature of the HOP is a simple redirection of employee benefits. The company redirects the contribution that they would have ordinarily put into an employee's retirement plan into the HOP and increases it so that the employee can save for a large tax-free down payment on a house. Private sector employers contribute a median 3 percent into retirement plans, and public sector contributions go as high as 7.5 percent of an employee's gross salary. The federal government and the states can make a 7.5 percent contribution the national standard, thereby encouraging corporations to raise their contributions to 7.5 percent. Contributions into the HOP are tax-free, as long as the savings are used to purchase a home. With the substantial advantage of the employer match and tax-free contributions, a couple can save enough for a down payment in just seven years.

Here is the real boost: working spouses can merge HOP accounts into one account and have $50,000 to $100,000 to make a down payment on their first home. The idea is to buy a home first and then save for retirement instead of renting.

Young people who start saving in a HOP account at age thirty, save for seven years, and buy a home at age thirty-seven will still have thirty years to save for retirement at age sixty-seven. With the large HOP down payment, people can reduce their housing costs up to $270 per month or more compared to renting and add that money to their retirement savings.

Table 3

Large Company or Public Sector HOP with a Starting Salary of $40,000

Year	Salary	Employee Contribution 7.5%	Employer Matching 7.5%		Annual Contribution	n Int. 5	Account Balance
1	$40,000	3,000	3,000	=	6,000	300	6,300
2	41,360	3,102	3,102	=	6,204	310	12,814
3	42,766	3,207	3,207	=	6,415	320	19,549
4	44,220	3,317	3,317	=	6,633	331	26,513
5	45,724	3,429	3,429	=	6,859	342	33,714
6	47,278	3,546	3,546	=	7,092	354	4,1160
7	48,886	3,666	3,666	=	7,333	366	48,849
8	50,548	3,791	3,791	=	7,582	374	56,820
9	52,267	3,920	3,920	=	7,840	392	65,022

Employer and employee contribute 7.5% each.

Table 3 shows employer and employee contributions of 7.5 percent each. The actual percentage contribution will vary according to each business or corporation. At present, government agencies contribute as much as 7.5 percent; this percentage needs to become the national standard for all 401(k) contributions, so that people can buy a home and have a comfortable retirement. Americans need to organize and demand that corporations and government provide a contribution of 7.5 percent of gross salary to their 401(k) retirement plan. Otherwise, few will have enough to retire, as people have already learned today.

Table 4
Contribution Rates to Retirement Plans Around the World

Denmark	11.8%
Australia	9.0%
Slovak Republic	9.0%
Poland	7.3%
Mexico	6.5%
United States	3.0% Median Private Sector Rate

Source: Jane White, "Things about 401(k) Plans We Need to Fix Now," The Huffington Post, March 21, 2013.

Clearly, the American people can hardly retire with such a paltry, shameful contribution rate of 3.0 percent, which is the median rate for the US private sector. Fidelity Investments, holding 16.2 million 401(k) accounts, reported that the average balance for people ages 60–69 was $198,600 in 2018. Who can retire safely with that?

With a starting salary of $40,000, and a 7.5 percent contribution into the HOP by both the employer and employee, a person can save $48,849 in just seven years in the HOP, which is more than enough for a 25 percent down payment on a home priced at $180,000. We need economic fairness if we want to buy a home and retire.

How the HOP Sets up Your Retirement Plan

When you take out a twenty-year mortgage, you save thousands of dollars in interest charges that you don't have to pay, compared to a thirty-year mortgage. Typically, bank quotes are only for fifteen-year or thirty-year mortgages; therefore, a young couple may well be tempted to go for the very lowest monthly payment, which is the thirty-year adjustable rate mortgage. Of course, we want only a fixed rate mortgage, so you don't end up with your house being foreclosed by the bank in hard times. Banks will lend on a fifteen-year or twenty-year fixed rate mortgage. You only have to ask. The interest rates shown in the example below are significantly higher than current rates, because economists project that mortgage interest rates will rise.

Table 5.
The Advantage of a Fifteen- or Twenty-Year Mortgage with a $100,000 Loan

Loan Term	Interest Rate	Monthly Payment	Interest Paid
15-year	5.67%	$826	$48,703
20-year	5.83%	$706	$69,598
30-year	6.00%	$600	$115,838

The HOP Advantage is more than a mere step up; it is a great leap forward in saving you money. The HOP enables you and your spouse to buy a home with a huge down payment, thereby eliminating thousands of dollars in mortgage interest payments over the life of the loan, depending on the interest rate. Over the years, the savings in interest for a fifteen-year mortgage when compared to a thirty-year mortgage is $67,135. The monthly savings in interest with a twenty-year mortgage is $46,240 when compared to a thirty-year mortgage. These savings can be added to your retirement savings account.

In fact, most people cannot retire securely and comfortably until they have paid off all their mortgages. If you rent when you retire, the monthly housing cost will consume 30 to 50 percent of your monthly retirement income.

How the Home Ownership Plan More Than Pays for Its Tax Exemptions

This analysis is structured to determine (1) the typical tax exemption for the HOP, (2) the amount of tax revenue from business and employee income taxes generated by the construction of a new home, and (3) other major factors involved in the net revenue gain to the US Treasury generated by the Home Ownership Plan. Table 6 shows tax exemptions for a HOP account, with contributions by both the employer and employee totaling 15 percent of gross salary. If the employer can only contribute 6 percent, the employee should choose to contribute 9 percent.

According to the National Association of Colleges and Employers, they found that for ten broad degree categories ranging from engineering to communications, 2018 graduates were projected to have an average salary of $51,000 to $56,000. An annual increase in salary is added at the rate of 3.4 percent each year, in the following table.

Table 6
Tax Exemptions for the Home Ownership Plan

Year	Gross Salary	Contributions Equal 15%	Tax Rate	Annual Tax Exemptions	Cumulative Tax Exemptions
1	$45,000	6,750	15%	1,012	$1,012
2	46,530	6,980	15%	1,047	2,059
3	48,112	7,217	15%	1,082	3,141
4	49,748	7,462	15%	1,119	4,260
5	51,539	7,730	25%	1,932	6,192
6	53,188	7,978	25%	1,994	8,186
7	54,997	8,249	25%	2,062	10,248

Note: Tax rates change so they must be updated.

Tax Revenues Generated by the Construction of a New Home

The amount of federal tax revenues generated by the home-building industry for single-family home construction is shown in Table 7.

Table 7
Fiscal Impacts of Building an Average Single-Family Housing Unit on the US Economy in 2005

Federal income taxes paid by employees $13,986
Federal income taxes paid by businesses $23,828
Total $37,814

Source: Abstracted from National Association of Home Builders estimates based primarily on data from the US Bureau of Economic Analysis. Note that 2005 was before the impact of the 2008 Great Recession.

Tax Revenue Gains that Will Be Generated by the Home Ownership Plan

The following analysis will show that the HOP will result in substantial tax revenue gains to the US Treasury. Table 7 shows that each newly constructed house generates an average of $37,814 in federal income taxes. As shown in Table 3, a HOP account with savings for seven years, in this example, tax exemptions would total $10,248. Thus, tax exemptions for a working couple could reach $20,496. Therefore, the US Treasury would be enriched by $17,318 for each home generated by the HOP ($37,814 minus $20,496 equals $17,318).

According to a Chicago Title and Trust national survey of the 1,237,000 new homes sold in 2005, approximately 578,916 were newly constructed homes, sold to first-time homebuyers. We can safely project that the popular Home Ownership Plan would boost those annual sales to 750,000 new homes per year. The US Treasury will see a net gain of $17,318 for each new home purchased by two HOP savers. $17,318 × 750,000 homes equals $12,988,500,000 per year, or approximately $13 billion per year.

The HOP Will Decrease Mortgage Interest Tax Deductions with No Change in Other Tax Laws

Table 8.
Mortgage Interest Tax Deductions (in Billions)

Deduction for mortgage interest on owner-occupied residences	2005	2006	2007	2008	2009	2005-2009
	$72.6	81.1	87.7	93.6	99.4	

Source: *Joint Committee on Taxation, US Congress*

An analysis by the US Congress Joint Committee on Taxation revealed that $52 billion in mortgage tax deductions were taken by households with incomes of $50,000 to $200,000 and above, whereas only $6 billion in deductions were taken by households with incomes of $49,000 or below. Home mortgage tax deductions not taken because the affluent will use the HOP to make such large down payments that they cannot take as large a deduction, which will result in a gain to the Treasury of an estimated $20 billion per year.

The HOP Will Reduce Federal and State Outlays for Unemployment Insurance Compensation by Billions of Dollars

Once the HOP is put in place, it will virtually eliminate housing-led recessions because people will cash out their HOP to buy a home, even during a recession, if they have stable jobs. Unemployment compensation not paid because of recession-proof housing and housing-related employment will add billions more to the Treasury. During the 2008 recession, federal and state outlays totaled $520 billion. The housing and housing related industries drive 25 percent of the economy, and 25 percent of $520 billion is $130 billion.

Table 9
Estimated Minimum Net Gains to the Treasury Generated by the Home Ownership Plan after a Period of Twenty Years, with 750,000 HOP Home Buyers Each Year

HOP-Generated Tax Revenues from Housing and Related Industries ($13 billion per year × 20 Years) = $260 billion
Tax Revenues from the Multiplier Effect ($8.7 billion per year × 20 Years) = $260 billion
Unemployment Compensation Not Taken over 20 Years = $130 billion
Mortgage Interest Deductions 20 billion × 20 Years = $400 billion
Total $1,050 Trillion

It should be noted that interest rates change from time to time in the examples shown above. The Congressional Joint Committee on Taxation will make the final analysis on this legislation and its benefits to the US Treasury.

Small Businesses and Single Person Firms Can Flourish by Giving the HOP to Themselves and to Their Employees, once It Is Legislated

Very few small businesses can afford to provide a 401(k) for twenty or thirty years. However, many small businesses can afford to pay 5 percent of gross salary into a HOP account for seven to nine years. The employer does not pay taxes on their contribution to the HOP, as a direct cash payment to the employee. The implementation of the HOP can, once again, increase loyalty between employers and employees, which will lead to a happier and more productive workplace. It should be noted that the totally new expansion of the HOP into businesses that employ about sixty million people will help to stabilize those businesses with happier, loyal employees and provide a whole new wave of first-time home buyers.

Providing More Federal Funds for Low-Income Home Buyers

A large share of these new revenues should be used to provide housing assistance to those who earn too little to participate in the HOP. Fully 50 percent of the net gain in revenues from the HOP should go into a national housing trust fund, which is *dedicated* to providing housing for very low-, low-, and moderate-income persons, including the homeless.

The National Housing Trust Fund, established in 2008, can also provide small efficiency apartments for the homeless. This is the best proven way to provide a secure foundation and help them get back on their feet and begin a new life, according to the results of programs in Utah and Colorado.

The HOP Produces Stable Home-Grown Jobs

When dollars are spent on housing and related industries, they largely stay in the domestic economy. You will never see a "Made in China" sign on an American house (although some materials are manufactured abroad). It is very important to have a large sector of secure manufacturing and construction skills consistently available in the American economy. After the 2008 housing bubble burst, thousands of construction workers lost their skills during unemployment.

Both the Left and the Right Can Happily Adopt This Bill

All lawmakers can support this bill, especially those with children, for this legislation is also called the "Parent Relief Bill," because your kids will not ask you for help with their down payment. This bill will create and sustain millions of jobs and generate billions of dollars to the Treasury. What lawmaker can be against that? This bill can stabilize 25 percent of the US economy with jobs that can't be outsourced. At a time when corporations are planning to eliminate up to 50 percent of our jobs using robots and information technology, the elite need to respond with intelligence to the justifiable worker outrage shown in the 2016 election cycle. The nation's workers realize that they have been substantially deprived of wage increases by large corporations for forty years. It is not a government problem.

As Martin Wolf, who reports on economics for the *Financial Times*, wrote in "Capitalism and Democracy: The Strain Is Showing," "To maintain legitimacy, economic policy must seek to promote the interests of the many not the few."

Chapter 8
Financing the New Towns for the Twenty-First Century

Governments print money to meet their needs; the United States did so in order to meet the threat of World War II. Catastrophic climate destruction of farming and sea life is another existential threat. Clearly, running out of oil and gasoline in thirty years is an existential threat. In 1973, when the OPEC countries raised the cost of oil and the cost of gasoline shot up from thirty-six cents to fifty-five cents per gallon, Americans were shocked. We woke up to the fact that we did not control oil prices and were totally dependent on our cars to drive out of the suburbs to work, shopping, and go anywhere. In 2010, military planners told us they could not guarantee that oil will be affordable or available in thirty years.

The rise of global warming is another existential threat, and it must be dealt with, because it has already cost $1.5 trillion from two hundred weather events, according to NOAA. We are throwing our money down a rat hole if we continue to ignore this destruction and expense. These simultaneous existential threats will require the US government and the private sector to spend trillions of dollars over the next thirty years. Financing new towns for the twenty-first century is a good way to deal with these threats, as well as supplying forty-seven million sustainable jobs that will be eliminated by robots and automation.

As noted above, institutional investors with $31 trillion under management stand ready to invest in renewable non-carbon energy, once the government takes the lead.

In her excellent book, *The Public Bank Solution*,[1] Ellen Brown describes how states can establish their own public banks, following the highly successful model of the Bank of North Dakota, which has operated for ninety years. States that establish their own banks can cut the cost of infrastructure projects in new towns nearly in half. They can do this by depositing their revenues in their own state bank and investing in safe state and municipal bonds.

Cutting the Cost of Infrastructure Projects Nearly in Half

In her book, Brown explains how states can save billions of dollars, while building the infrastructure, as follows:

> Assume the bank invested in municipal bonds that paid it 4 percent interest, and the state was paying 4 percent interest on its own state bonds. Revenue from the municipal bonds would be sufficient to pay the interest on the state bonds, so the state's own debt would still be effectively interest free. By depositing its revenues and investing on Wall Street, the state is giving this potential income stream away.[2]

Brown cites a good example of how this is done:

> Tom Hagan, who pays taxes in Maine, maintains that infrastructure costs could be slashed by this device risk-free. In a December 2011 letter to the editor of the *Portland Press Herald*, he maintained that there is no need for a publicly-owned bank to invest in risky ventures. It could just buy safe municipal bonds. Using the example of the Maine turnpike project, he showed that this simple measure could cut the cost of local projects nearly in half:

Improvements are funded by bonds issued by the Maine Turnpike Authority, which collects the principal amounts, then pays the bonds back with interest.

Over time, interest payments add up to about the original principle, doubling the cost of turnpike improvements and the tolls that must be collected to pay for them. The interest money is shipped out of state to Wall Street banks.

Why not keep the interest money here in Maine, to the benefit of Mainers? This could be done by creating a state owned bank. State funds now deposited in low-or no interest checking accounts would instead be deposited in the state bank.

Those funds would be used to buy up the authority bonds and municipal bonds issued by the Maine Bond Bank. Since all interest payments would flow into the state treasury, we would end up paying half what we now pay for our roads, bridges and schools. North Dakota has profited from a state-owned bank for 90 years. Why not Maine?[3]

Twenty States Have Introduced Bills to Form Public Banks

Twenty states have now introduced bills of one sort or another to form state-owned banks, according to Brown, who advises state governments on how to get those bills implemented and where to find money for start-up capital. She also explains how we need to rein in Wall Street and the threat to the public from investors gambling on derivatives. The private sector banking industry needs to invest billions in the race to provide energy for the nation before we run out of oil. If they refuse to do so, they are accelerating the possible total collapse of the economic system, including their own banks. Again, they will be stranded capitalists.

The Reconstruction Finance Corporation: The Public Financial Institution that Pulled Us Out of the Depression and Funded World War II

Brown describes this little-known public financing institution, which can be used again to build new towns of the twenty-first century:

In the 1930s and 1940s, the Reconstruction Finance Corporation (RFC) was America's largest corporation and the world's largest banking organization. It was a remarkable credit machine that allowed the government to fund the New Deal and World War II without turning to Congress or the taxpayers for appropriations. It generated massive infrastructure and development all across the country, while turning a profit to the government. Yet this sterling model for what might be done is rarely mentioned in the media today. The RFC was not a commercial bank and did not issue loans against deposits.[4]

The RFC funded its loans with bonds:

> The bonds soaked up money sitting idle in the economy and put it to work building infrastructure and creating jobs, and it did it all without tapping into the federal budget or raising taxes. The bonds were paid off with the proceeds from the projects funded by the loans (called "self-funding" loans). The RFC funded the rebuilding of the country while at the same time turning a profit for the government.[5] After we build solar banks, wind farms, and nuclear mini-reactors, the sales of energy that they produce will pay off the bonds for construction.

Franklin D. Roosevelt continually enlarged and added functions to the RFC in order to meet the financial and economic crisis of the times. The RFC Act of 1932 provided the RFC with capital stock of $500 million, subscribed by the United States of America. With government-owned stock, it had the authority to extend credit up to $1.5 billion. This was subsequently increased to $3 billion, a substantial sum at the time, since in 1932 the entire budget of the US government was only $4.6 billion. Beyond the initial $500 million, the RFC raised capital by issuing its own debentures, a form of bond. The RFC loaned or invested more than $40 billion. A small part of this came from its initial capitalization. The rest was borrowed from the Treasury and the public. These loans did not cost the government but actually produced a profit, earning a total net income of $690,017,232 on RFC's normal lending functions (omitting such things as extraordinary grants for wartime). The RFC generated funds for roads, bridges, dams, post offices, universities, electrical power, mortgages, farms, and much more; it funded all this while actually making money for the government.[6]

There are currently over 30 trillions of investor dollars in the US economy which can be called upon to build the energy needs of the country and create a new manufacturing base using automation and new towns for the twenty-first century.

Chapter 9
The Urgency to Mobilize and Avoid Future Damage

The 2018 Intergovernmental Panel on Climate Change Report is a wake-up call to the world that we are in great jeopardy. Climate change is already affecting people's lives, livelihoods, and ecosystems around the world with historically unheard-of destruction, causing massive migrations and loss of lives. It was projected that we only have twelve years in which to avoid tipping points, such as the release of methane across nine million square miles across the northern hemisphere and the melting of large parts of Antarctica are threatening to raise sea levels by 11 feet.

The IPCC report, written by ninety-one researchers and editors from forty countries, citing more than six thousand scientific documents, was released on October 8, 2018; it provides details on the challenge before us to keep the earth from warming beyond 1.5 degrees C.

Major cities, such as New York, Miami, Tokyo, London, Mumbai, Manila, New Orleans, Osaka, Shanghai, and Jakarta, Indonesia, risk disastrous flooding from sea level rise, unless we stop burning fossil fuels. The average global temperature has risen 1 degree C over the last 115 years. The sea water is so warm that hurricanes and typhoons have reached Category 5 with sustained wind speeds of 156 mph, which sweeps houses off their foundations, as it did in Mexico Beach, Florida, in 2018. Astonishing rainfall levels of twenty or more inches in twenty-four hours are causing catastrophic flooding and damaging homes, highways, and food crops in the Midwest. These new and historic rainfall levels are caused by tropical storms and hurricanes, and they cause rivers to overflow their banks. During El Nino years, the damage is even more costly, as it warms the water more.

We have already seen what a 1 degree C rise in temperature can do; that should be enough to convince any reasonable person that the time for sleepwalking is over. We still may have time to stop global warming at 1.5 degrees C, if we take bold action now and lead the world as a nation, but first we must overcome our initial inertia and mobilize with hard-driving action. This is no time for moderation as some corporate narratives would suggest.

The important IPCC report was virtually ignored by MSNBC, FOX News, and other national media. CNN, with host Brook Baldwin, gave a five-minute report, and that was all I saw on TV. The editorial boards of the major news media apparently do not have a grasp of the gravity of our situation and what needs to be done about global warming. PBS produced a documentary called *Sinking Cities*, with Tokyo, Miami, and New York as examples.

The IPCC's report warns that 2 degrees C will bring a staggering increase in heat waves, more powerful storms, and rising sea levels that are already battering people and economies around the world and will expose hundreds of millions of people to displacement, loss of property, water shortages, and increased poverty. The good news is that humankind can take action and avoid some of these disasters, as we shall see.

The executive branch and Congress must understand this crisis, realize we must take action, and approach the problem with extreme urgency; it's the only chance we have to protect our children and our grandchildren from unbearable destruction from climate disasters and a fearful future. We must take the actions described in this book or come up with even better ideas and policies, or we will perish as a species. There is a path to take, with great haste and urgency. That is the Good News. So, let us proceed to the Good News.

The Mobilization of the Nation

If we continue to sleepwalk into the future with business as usual, we are guaranteed to have total economic system collapse, and our children will be living in a brutish and dangerous world. In order to deal with these existential threats, the nation must mobilize on a scale greater than we did in World War II. There are some immediate steps that we can take to dramatically reduce carbon emissions.

For example, in just thirty years, we will have to produce about 1,500 gigawatts of electricity from solar, wind power, and safe nuclear power. We will need to eliminate coal burning by replacing it with non-carbon-producing energy. When the wind doesn't blow and the sun does not shine, we can have safe molten salt thorium-fueled nuclear reactors to supply energy to a region 24/7. The lack of battery storage issue has been solved (except for vehicles).

We will need to build rapid transit systems, with non-carbon energy, in the suburbs to reduce the use of gas-powered automobiles by up to 66 percent; we also need to let millions of people work at home, using computers to move data instead of moving people in autos. People working at home can still fill quotas and meet deadlines.

We will need to produce about a hundred million automobiles that operate with non-carbon electricity. We will need to build new towns with built-in rapid transit systems, affordable housing, and sustainable livelihoods for forty-seven million people whose existing jobs will be eliminated by robots and automation.

We will need to immediately stop eating so much beef and reduce the emissions of bovine methane, which is the number two cause of CO_2 emissions. (As Jeremy Rifkin said, "Nobody wants to talk about it.") Meatless hamburgers have already been made from plants. We need not sacrifice our hamburgers.

Our children are telling us that stopping disastrous climate change is non-negotiable, for the future environment they'd have to live in will be terrifying if we do not act now. We can no longer allow the love of money to be greater than our love for God's good will, his beautiful creation, and the love of our own children and grandchildren. Not to mention the animals and plants who God values, even if many humans have not learned to appreciate them. The lengths we go to avoid dealing with global warming is stupefying. The measured scientific evidence is overwhelming.

Now, we are confronted with potential disasters as seen personally by our own senses. Seeing is believing, they say. Yet we, as a society and a civilization, do not act upon what we know. Frank Sheed, in his book, *Theology and Sanity*,[7] throws some light on our problem. Sheed observes that there are three defects of the human intellect:

Truths it simply does not know. [In the case of climate change, this is astonishing ignorance.]

Truths it knows but does not advert to. [This is when we know something is true but we do not realize it enough to take action.]

Truths it knows and adverts to but does not comprehend. [This is when the reality of our problem is so immense that we have trouble grasping the danger of our situation because the reality is so hard to even process.]

As Carl Jung said, "Man can only handle so much reality." Now that we are in the depths of our calamity, we must see the truth, realize the truth, and act upon the truth. We need to fully comprehend it and mobilize to take action. We must process the truth, and then we'll find that the best way to deal with the awful truth is to take action. Trusting in God's providential action, we can move forward because he is with us, as he has given us the power to be co-creators with him. He is with us. That is our strength, and that is what gives us our intellectual know how and the power to love and to use our imaginations to move forward.

As Pope Francis has pointed out, we are *part* of the living environment; we are not outside observers. We are embedded in living creation as part of the whole. God has given us the authority and power to be good stewards of the living environment, our only home: Earth. There is no alternative planet within billions of light years that is habitable. We must take care of the incredibly beautiful Spaceship Earth and its inhabitants, and then we can "have life and have it more abundantly," as offered by Christ (John 10:10).

In order to mobilize the nations, we will need to draw upon the spiritual power of divine grace and then trust in God that we can save ourselves, our planet, our sea life, and all of God's creation. Not to do so is to continue a dive into total evil and self-annihilation. That is unthinkable. To begin the process in America and other nations, the press and the media must educate everyone about our life-threatening situation and explain how to take positive action immediately. We will need the continual help of the news media to show our forward progress and reduce widespread anxiety.

In order to proceed with vigor, intelligence, and vision, we will need a wise president, with a talented cabinet and a super functional Congress, with a majority having a factual understanding of our national threats, a visionary plan for the future, and the wisdom to fund what is needed to prevail.

The federal government needs to develop a national energy production and transportation plan, utilizing planners, architects, and engineers of all kinds. Their primary goals will be to rapidly create non-carbon energy and to rapidly reduce the use of fossil fuels, with the understanding that thirty years is a short time period to replace oil throughout the economy. We will need to plant millions of trees globally. We will need to mobilize the nation with greater urgency than we have ever seen before. We will need to rapidly scale up many sources of electricity and biofuels in order to meet the nation's needs.

Scaling up Biofuels for Aircraft

It is important to note that chemical fuels, such as ethanol, are required to provide the powerful energy that can lift large jet planes off the runway. I was told by a jet engine engineer that the Russians flew some of their airplanes on vodka during the Cold War. They called them "flying restaurants." Clearly, we will need to modify our luxurious lifestyles and use commercial aviation less often. Including the air shipment of goods and passengers, there were eighty-seven thousand US flights per day in 2018.

Ethanol fuel is the most common biofuel produced worldwide. Alcohol fuels, including vodka, are produced by fermentation of sugars derived mostly from wheat, corn, sugar beets, and sugar cane. In the United States, sugar cane and corn are the most popular plants to produce ethanol. Sugar from wood (cellulose) can also be used for fuel. The process for producing ethanol from cellulose, invented by Marshall Medoff and his engineers has a 77% reduction in greenhouse gases when burned. This method of fuel production needs to be scaled up with a speed never seen before.

Electric car production will take a long time to scale up; they also require the scaling up of their own non-carbon electricity. While burning ethanol increases carbon dioxide, ethanol is produced from plants that have taken in carbon dioxide in order to produce its sugars. When the burning of the fuel releases carbon dioxide, it is roughly equal to what was taken in beforehand (with burning fossil fuels, there is no such equalizer).

To further reduce carbon dioxide, we need to change our lifestyles by not flying so much, using rapid transit, and creating systems so that millions of people can work at home. Again, we can move data instead of moving people around. Supervision and oversight of a worker's production can be measured by the amount of successful output on a weekly basis. There should be no problem with worker-owned cooperative corporations, for they are their own bosses and are under peer group pressure to perform well for all.

Electric Rapid Transit Systems for the Sprawling Suburbs

One of the best ways to reduce the number of fossil fuel-burning cars on the road is to build mass transit in the existing suburbs. We can develop buses that run on electricity or ethanol. We can use ten-seat vans to pick up and disperse people from main terminals and to their final destination. Such a system would enable a family to operate with only one car instead of two or three cars. A family can use one car for emergencies, grocery shopping, and long-distance travel.

There are 250 million cars on the road today; we could reduce that number by one-third, or 75 million gas-guzzlers and CO_2 emitters, rather quickly, by having people work at home.

Scaling up Wind Power

Wind power is now the least-expensive electricity source, with a levelized cost (including capital and operating cost) at 8.2 cents per kilowatt hour. As cited above, we can have saturation wind power on wind farms because they can be spaced so as not to interfere with each other's operation. Also, we can build enough capacity to supply the whole nation if we should decide to do so, although we will want to use solar as well, with large farms of photovoltaic cells, and safe liquid fluoride thorium reactors to produce electricity around the clock, 24/7 when the wind doesn't blow.

One of the great advantages of wind turbines is that they can be placed on fields where food or biofuel crops are grown, to the benefit of farmers. Also, as you may have noticed while driving, wind turbines can be placed on the right-of-way of highways.

The states with the most wind power include Texas, northward up through the Plains states and to North Dakota. Also, the entire West

Coast and East Coast have sufficient wind to install wind turbines offshore in the ocean.

Scaling up Solar Thermal Power Plants

Solar thermal power plants receive the most sun in the Southwest states. Solar thermal plants use a huge array of mirrors to focus the sun's rays on heating a liquid in a high tower. The heat produces steam, which drives turbine generators to produce electricity. This requires a substantial amount of acreage; such energy plants are best suited for the desert. America's vast deserts can produce a prodigious amount of electricity. With direct current transmission lines, electricity can be sent to major cities in the Midwest and Northeast, 2,400 miles away, with only a 15 percent loss of energy.

Scaling up Algae Biofuel Production

As cited above, Exxon Mobil is developing a process to produce biofuel from algae in large tanks. The algae do not have to be harvested, because the oils can be scooped up without harming the plant. Exxon Mobil could scale up this work using unproductive farmland.

Scaling up Battery Storage Systems

As cited above, about twenty thousand highly motivated engineers must work on the design of electric storage batteries that can be scaled up to meet the nation's electricity needs for cars.

Accelerating Research and Production of Liquid Fluoride Thorium Reactors to Produce Electricity 24/7

Scientists and engineers have been working on the perfection of a safe nuclear reactor that does not have a fuel that can be easily used in nuclear weapons. Researchers in the United States, Canada, Germany, France, Japan, and China are working to develop a superior Generation IV nuclear reactor. This endeavor needs to be accelerated with federal funding for

R&D from all these nations, working together and sharing their results, insights, and modifications.

In *Super Fuel: Thorium the Green Energy Source for the Future*,[1] Richard Martin provides a strong case for building this safe nuclear reactor. His major case is as follows:

> Because as I demonstrate in *Super Fuel*, the book, renewables are not going to solve our problem in the time scales that we need it—in other words, in the next 30 to 50 years. Solar and wind and so on are just not going to be at large enough scales and at the prices to really replace a significant fraction of fossil fuel-based energy in the time frames we need.
>
> So we are talking about two different risks, here: the risks associated with an innovative form of nuclear power based on a very abundant and safe material versus the risk of a three-degree-Celsius, let's say, rise in global temperatures over the next 50 years, within, you know, my son's lifetime. So, as a society, I don't think we are very good at calculating risk. And so to hone in on these pretty technical issues of, well, there might be some very small proliferation risk with thorium, there's no question that thorium-liquid fueled reactors can be used to consume the existing waste from conventional reactors.[2]

Martin points out that molten salt thorium reactor experiments were conducted at Oak Ridge National Laboratory in Tennessee from 1959 until 1973. It was completely proven, but then development had been interrupted by World War II; uranium was much better for making bombs. That was when the government pushed thorium fuel aside in favor of using uranium.

Martin also cites the advantages regarding radioactive waste when using a thorium reactor: In a liquid thorium reactor, the core is liquid. You can continually process waste, even from existing conventional reactors, into forms that are much smaller in terms of volume, and the radioactivity drops off much, much quicker. That means that we can safely store much smaller quantities of radioactive waste in geologically preferred deep earth depositories.

With thorium reactors, radioactivity declines after a few hundred years, as opposed to tens of thousands of years with uranium. So, yes, we would need to store waste in a depository deep underground, but the volume is a tenth of 1 percent of the comparable volume of waste from a conventional reactor. We also have all that waste from our existing nuclear submarine fleet, just sitting around with no plan for its disposal. We will need to make storage a top priority.

The Cost Factor

Martin writes, "Ralph Moir, a scientist formerly associated with Lawrence Livermore National Laboratory, in 2002, calculated that the cost of electricity from a LFTR to be 3.8 cents per kilowatt-hour, less than coal at 4.2 cents."[3]

He points out that theft of uranium-233 from a liquid thorium reactor would require retrieving it somehow from the reactor. It's not sitting in a warehouse somewhere. And because this is a self-contained liquid fuel system, there is no point at which you can divert the material. To be able to obtain that uranium-233 material, you would somehow have to breach the reactor, shut it down, separate out the fissionable material, and escape, evading electron surveillance and armed assault by our police and armed forces.

Also, as Martin points out in *Super Fuel*, "Even if someone manages to do that theft, the uranium-233 is contaminated with yet another isotope, U-232, which is one of the nastiest substances in the universe, and it makes handling and processing and separating U-232 virtually impossible, even for a sophisticated nuclear power lab, much less a rogue nation, or terrorist group or someone of that ilk. So, good luck with that."[4]

We may conclude that diverting liquid thorium to build nuclear weapons there is really not a problem. Bad people would go after easier-to-get uranium. There is much less waste to be deposited underground, and it uses existing uranium waste in its process.

Martin describes what it will take to mobilize the production of LFTRs. First, it would take a sense of urgency; people must recognize that the destruction from global warming is rapidly closing in on us. The future is happening now, with California wildfires, rising sea levels, historical flooding of whole cities, crop losses from excessive rainfall, and hurricanes at the Category 5 levels, with wind speeds of up to 175 mph.

We also need research and development to get LFTRs approved and funded. The president will have to order the Nuclear Regulatory Commission to expedite its licensing process so that the period from application to final approval is less than two years.

We should plan to construct 250- to 400-megawatt LFTRs, which can be assembled in large plants like a Boeing aircraft (the aircraft manufacturer assembles forty-seven 737 jets in thirty days).

In 2018, the total US electricity generating capacity was about 1,000 gigawatts. LFTRs can supply 50 percent of that need faster than any other source, if we expedite the processes for all of them. According to Martin, it would cost $600 billion to build twenty-four hundred 250-megawatt machines, for 600,000 megawatts of power. That $600 billion is just one-half the $1.2 trillion that we are spending on defense, intelligence, and Homeland Security in one year (see chapter 5). What a bargain to defend the nation from total destruction by global warming. However, we have just twelve years to accomplish most of our task. LFTR's can be built by the late 2020's. We can supply 50 percent of our electrical energy with LFTRs, and 50 percent from solar, wind, geothermal, and so on.

A national energy plan would consider all these components and scale up energy production, with financing from private investors and government, and work with companies in the private sector to hasten their construction.

Building New Towns for the Twenty-First Century

Producing solar, wind, LFTRs, and biofuels on a large scale will require a manufacturing base to create and assemble the components necessary, for photovoltaic cells, wind turbines, nuclear reactors, and biofuel plants. These proposed new towns will also manufacture all the basic necessities of life, such as affordable housing, heating and cooling equipment, furniture, agriculture, supermarkets, household appliances, house maintenance, apparel stores, electrification, and entertainment centers. The major products of these new towns would be solar, wind, and nuclear energy. Products can be sold to other towns in order to buy luxury items that a new town doesn't want to (or can't) produce.

Some new towns will produce steel, aluminum, copper, and other basic items which are supplied to manufacturing plants, producing life's necessities, including transportation vehicles. The concept is to build a more self-sufficient America, so we can afford to buy what is made in America, by using automation to our advantage, instead of cheap foreign labor. About 30 percent of our occupations will be replaced by automation, so we will need to create eighty-three million sustainable livelihoods, as cited above, including jobs for the growing population. By using a new town planning framework, we can use the latest ideas for creating a better, healthier life rather than simply earning money for a living or to produce goods to maximize profit-making. What a wonderful and highly creative process to lift our spirits with hope and joy.

The vast majority of working families need a 1,500-square-foot apartment with three bedrooms and two bathrooms and ample storage space. Such apartments, or homes, can be built in an affordable price range for working families at about $180,000 in 2019. This will be affordable housing for the middle class if we use the Home Ownership Plan described in chapter 7. As a nation, we need to go back to the days of building affordable housing, since working people in our large cities cannot afford houses that now cost $300,000 to $1,000,000. Many rural areas are having the same difficulty. However, we cannot build more sprawling suburbs. We will need to build vertically, and that means new designs for human living and recreation, not just cold high-rises. As described in chapter 2, we can build twelve-story low-rises with laminated wood beams and columns with new socializing spaces designed by architects.

Building Vertically Is Needed in Order to Conserve Agricultural Land

As the population of the world increases to 9 billion, agricultural land will be needed for food crops and biofuels. We will need to build energy-efficient low-rise housing with new features for better living and socializing. For example, we can build low-rises that provide horizontal space for playgrounds, parks, outdoor cooking, parties, and greenhouses to grow plants and herbs. Restaurants and supermarkets will be nearby to reduce travel time and the cost to obtain food.

Time Is of the Essence

The executive branch and an informed Congress must lead the nation's corporations to understand that in order to achieve the goals cited above, and finally replace fossil fuels, we need a unified national effort that we've never experienced before. Most of the easy-to-get oil will be consumed in about twenty years; we probably reached peak oil in 2006, and the pending decline in US oil, due to increased global consumption, creates the necessity for immediate action. For it is not only the military that will run out of oil in just thirty years but the entire domestic economic system. There are some who will try to deny these facts; however, today's circumstances cannot be avoided with magical thinking. Alex Kuhlman said it best, as quoted above, and it's well-worth restating:

However, with an acute lack of awareness, of time, knowledge, capital, energy, political will, and international collaboration, it is difficult to see how business can continue as usual. A new path must be chosen to conserve the underlying fossil fuel base required to develop and implement sustainable energy sources capable of running even a substantial fraction of countries such as the USA. Otherwise, we may lack the tools to move forward to replace a fluid so cheap, abundant and versatile.[5]

Mobilization Time Is at Hand

We are truly challenged to undertake nation building at home, with all of us united to achieve the goals cited above, as never before. Divisions and factions need to be set aside as we work together, with a new-found love, for our survival and our children's good future life. We will need oil, while it is still affordable, to build a new economic platform more to our liking. We must be aware that our situation is challenging; we have to join together, with a new social consciousness, to provide for our future. This is the spiritual, intellectual, and physical work of our lifetimes. We dare not fail, and we cannot fail, if we work together with spirit.

Hope for Our Future

While we face many perils, we can take hope that our situation gives us an opportunity to build an economic system and a society that embraces the transcendent and universal values of truth, goodness, justice, and pursuit of the common good. We need to embrace these values and reject the ideas of relativism, which says, "My values are as good as your values; I will do want I want." This is a selfish, egoistic, and destructive attitude. So I must appeal to a higher authority: God's Son, who has taught us the values of truth, goodness, and love for each other. If we continue down the path of rejecting the universal values of love for one another, we will endure greater global suffering, loss of dear ones, loss of hope, and loss of love.

Now, we have the challenge to change and the great opportunity to change for the better and provide a whole new way of happier living. The human spirit has been through two World Wars and has survived and thrived. Now, we can design a better future for ourselves and our children. While God does not interfere with our free will, be it good or bad, He does grant us the faculties of intellect and will to make good choices and be co-creators with him. That is how all human inventions are generated, in my understanding. Therein lies our greatest hope to build a better future together and advance the forward days of humankind. For God is in charge, not humans, and He is all powerful, kind, and merciful. When we undertake the task of stopping global warming and the destruction of lives, property, animals, phytoplankton, and all sea life, we will be working to be good stewards of God's own beautiful creation. For that reason, I believe that God will provide us with the inventions, the tools, the time, and the will to make his creation beautiful again. We now have all of the basic technology to slow and eventually stop global warming. We now just need to take bold action to implement our solutions. So let us mobilize as never before and get to work; we need to refocus on our life's goals. For as Thomas Merton famously wrote, "Love seeks only one thing: the good of the beloved."[6] It is time to unite in brotherly and sisterly love, cast away our divisions, acknowledge our dangerous situation, mobilize the nation and get started toward a sustainable future for all humankind.

References

Introduction

1   Glikson, Andrew, "The Arctic Climate Tipping Point: Methane and the Future of the Biosphere," Global Research, April 29, 2018.
2   The IPCC Report, OECD/IEA, 2018.
3   Osborne, Michael, and Carl Benedikt Frey, "The Future of Employment: How Susceptible Are Jobs to Computerization?" The Oxford Martin Programme on Technology and Employment, September 17, 2013.
4   Harvard Joint Center on Housing Studies, "The State of the Nation's Housing 2018," Harvard University.
5   Parthemore, Christine, and John Nagl, *Fueling the Future Force*, Center for a New American Security, 2010.
6   Kelton, Stephanie, "Stephanie Kelton Has the Biggest Idea in Washington," Huffington Post, May 20, 2018.
7   Smith, Adam, "2017 U.S. billion-dollar weather and climate disasters: a historic year in context," *Climate Watch*, January 8, 2018.

Chapter 1
Worker-Owned Cooperatives: Why They Are Good

1   Mondragon Cooperative Corporation Annual Report 2014.
2   Roy, *We Build the Road as We Travel*, p. 13.
3   Wikipedia, Mondragon Sales.
4   Morrison, *We Build the Road as We Travel*, p. 10.
5   The *Economist*, "Germany's Banking System: Old Fashioned but in Favor," November 10, 2012.

Chapter 2
The Creation of Satellite New Towns

1   Harvard, "The State of the Nation's Housing 2018."
2   Kelton, "Stephanie Kelton Has the Biggest Idea in Washington."
3   Hutchins, Gareth, "Largest Ever Group of Investors Call for More Action to Meet Paris Targets," *The Guardian*, December 10, 2018.
4   Meyerson, Harold, "In Corporations, It's Owner Take All," *Washington Post*, August 26, 2014.
5   Meadows, Donella, and Dennis Meadows, *The Limits to Growth*, Washington DC, Potomac Associates, 1972.

Chapter 3
Oil Will Be Unaffordable in Thirty Years

1   U.S. Joint Forces Command, "The Joint Operating Environment," March 15, 2010.
2   Parthemore and Nagl, *Fueling the Future Force.*
3   Ibid.
4   Ibid.
5   The International Energy Agency Annual Report 2012, OECD/IEA, 2012.
6   Rifkin, Jeremy, *The Third Industrial Revolution*, Palgrave McMillan, 2011, p. 17.
7   Ibid.
8   Klare, Michael T., *The Race for What's Left: The Global Scramble for the World's Last Resources*, Metropolitan Books, 2012.
9   Ibid.
10 Ibid.
11 Gilding, Paul, *The Great Disruption: Why Climate Change Will Transform the World*, Bloomsbury Publishing, 2011.
12 Kuhlman, Alex, "Peak Oil and the Collapse of Commercial Aviation," *AIRWAYS*, 2006.

Chapter 4
Superabundant Energy Provides Wealth for All

1   Cardwell, Diane, "Solar and Wind Start to Win on Price vs. Conventional Fuels," *New York Times*, November 23, 2014.
2   Jacobson, Mark Z., and Christine Archer, "Saturation Wind Power Potential and Its Implications for Wind Energy," National Academy of Sciences, 2012.

3   Bright Source, Ivanpah project. (See Bright Source on the internet).
4   Diamondis, Peter, and Steven Kotler, *Abundance: The Future Is Better Than You Think*, New York, Free Press, 2012, p. 169.
5   Ibid.
6   Kurzweil AI/Accelerating Intelligence News, "A Solar Energy Storage Cell that Works at Night," July 3, 2015.
7   Reuter News staff, "The World's Largest Investors, with $22.5 Trillion, Call for Climate Change Action," November 20, 2012.
8   Norris, Vivian, "Here Comes the Sun: Tunisia to Energize Europe," Huffington Post, January 28, 2012.
9   Morrison, *We Build the Road as We Travel*, p. 10.
10 Pope Francis, *The Joy of the Gospels*, Erlanger, Kentucky, Dynamic Catholic Institute, 2014, p. 52.

Chapter 5
How to Create Millions of Livelihoods

1   Rosane, Olivia, "Electric Vehicle Sales More Than Double in 2017," Eco Watch, May 30, 2018.
2   Fuller, Buckminster, *Operating Manual for the Spaceship Earth*, Southern Illinois University Press, March 1969.
3   Ibid.
4   Ibid.
5   Ibid.
6   Raworth, Kate, *Doughnut Economics: Seven Ways to Think Like a 21st Century Economist*, White River Junction, Vermont, Chelsea Green Publishing, 2017.
7   Gates, Robert, "Blasts Wars Like Iraq and Afghanistan," *Palm Beach Post*, February 26, 2011.
8   Hellman, Christopher, "The Real National Security Budget: The Figure No One Wants You to See," Tom Dispatch.com, March 2, 2011.
9   Pollin, Robert, and Heidi Garrett-Peltier, "Don't Buy the Spin: How Cutting the Pentagon's Budget Could Boost the Economy," *The Nation*, May 28, 2012.
10 Barnet, Richard J., "Reflections: After the Cold War," *New Yorker*, January 1, 1990.
11 Sachs, Jeffrey, Sustainable Development Solutions Network, 2018 SDG Index and Dashboards, A Global Initiative for the United Nations.
12 Islamic Declaration on Climate Change, United Nations, August 18, 2015.
13 Pope Francis, *Encyclical on Climate Change & Inequality*, London, Melville House, 2015.
14 Ibid.
15 Rohr, Richard, *A Spring within Us: A Book of Daily Meditations*, CAC Publishing, 2016.

Chapter 6
The Advancement of Social Consciousness

1   *Washington Post*, "Muslim Leaders Support Islamic Declaration on Climate Change," August 18, 2015.
2   Pope Francis, *Encyclical on Climate Change and Inequality—On Care for Our Common Home*, London, Melville House, July 2015, p. 86.
3   Ibid, p. vii.
4   Rohr, Richard, *Immortal Diamond: The Search for Our True Selves*, London, Society for Promotion of Christian Knowledge, 2015.

Chapter 7
The Home Ownership Plan

1   Fleming, Duane E., Home Ownership Plan legislation, ("Restore the American Dream Act"), HR 3557, 2007.
2   Reich, Robert, "Almost 80% of US Workers Live from Paycheck to Paycheck. Here's Why." *The Guardian*, July 29, 2018.

Chapter 8
Financing the New Towns for the Twenty-First Century

1   Brown, Ellen, *The Public Bank Solution, From Austerity to Prosperity*, Baton Rouge, Louisiana, Third Millennium Press, 2013.
2   Ibid., p. 376
3   Ibid., pp. 376–377.
4   Ibid.
5   Ibid.
6   Ibid.

Chapter 9
The Urgency to Mobilize and Avoid More Damage

1   Sheed, Frank, *Theology and Sanity*, San Francisco, Ignatius Press, 1946, 1948, 1993, p. 44.
2   Martin, Richard, *Super Fuel: Thorium the Green Energy Source for the Future*, New York, St. Martins Griffin, 2012.
3   Ibid.
4   Ibid.

5   Kuhlman, Alex, "Peak oil and the collapse of commercial aviation", AIRWAYS Magazine, 2006.
6   Brown, *The Public Bank Solution, From Austerity to Prosperity.*
7   Sheed, *Theology and Sanity.*

Bibliography

Barnet, Richard J., "Reflections: After the Cold War," *New Yorker* (January 1, 1990).

Bright Source, Ivanpah Project. (See the internet.)

Brown, Ellen, *The Public Bank Solution, From Austerity to Prosperity* (Baton Rouge, Louisiana, Third Millennium Press, 2013).

Cardwell, Diane, "Solar and Wind Start to Win on Price vs. Conventional Fuels," *New York Times* (November, 23, 2014).

Diamondis, Peter and Kotler, Steven, *Abundance: The Future Is Better than You Think* (New York, Free Press, 2012), p. 169.

Fleming, Duane E., "The Home Ownership Plan" legislation (A.K.A. "Restore the American Dream Act"), with Representative Robert Wexler, HR 3557 (2007).

Francis, Pope Francis, *Encyclical on Climate Change & Inequality* (London, Melville House, 2015.

Fuller, Buckminster, *Operating Manual for the Spaceship Earth* (Southern Illinois University Press, March 1969).

Glikson, Andrew, "The Arctic Climate Tipping Point: Methane and the Future of the Biosphere" (Global Research, April 29, 2018).

Gilding, Paul, *The Great Disruption: Why Climate Change Will Transform the World* (Bloomsbury Publishing, 2011).

Hellman, Christopher, "The Real National Security Budget: The Figure No One Wants You to See" (Tom Dispatch.com, March 2, 2011).

Jacobson, Mark Z. and Christine Archer, "Saturation Wind Power Potential and Its Implications for Wind Energy (National Academy of Sciences, 2012).

Kelton, Stephanie, "Stephanie Kelton Has the Biggest Idea in Washington" (Huffington Post, May 20, 2018).

Kirzweil AI/Accelerating Intelligence News, "A Solar Energy Storage Cell that Works at Night" (July 3, 2015).

Klare, Michael, *The Race for What's Left: The Global Scramble for the World's Last Resources* (Metropolitan Books, 2012).

Kuhlman, Alex, "Peak Oil and the Collapse of Commercial Aviation" (*Airways*, 2006).

Martin, Richard, *Super Fuel: Thorium the Green Energy Source for the Future* (New York, St. Martin's Griffin, 2012).

Meadows, Donella, and Dennis Meadows, *The Limits to Growth* (Potomac Associates, Washington DC, 1972).

Meyerson, Harold, "In Corporations, It's Owner Take All (*Washington Post*, August 26, 2014).

Mondragon Cooperative Corporation, Annual Report, 2014.

Morrison, Roy, *We Build the Road as We Travel* (Philadelphia, New Society Publishers, 1991), p. 13.

Norris, Vivian, "Here Comes the Sun: Tunisia to Energize Europe (Huffington Post, January 28, 2012).

Osborne, Michael, and Carl Benedikt Frey, "The Future of Employment: How Susceptible Are Jobs to Computerization?" (Oxford Martin Programme on Technology and Employment, September 17, 2013).

Parthemore, Christine, and John Nagl, *Fueling the Future Force* (Center for a New American Security, 2010).

Pollin, Robert, and Heidi Garret-Peltier, "Don't Buy the Spin: How Cutting the Pentagon Budget Can Boost the Economy," *The Nation*, May 28, 2012.

Raworth, Kate, *Doughnut Economics: 7 Ways to Think Like a 21st Century Economist* (Chelsea Green Publishing, White River Junction, Vermont, 2017).

Reich, Robert, "Almost 80% of US Workers Live from Paycheck to Paycheck. Here's Why" (*The Guardian*, July 29, 2018).

Rifkin, Jeremy, *The Third Industrial Revolution* (Palgrave McMillan, 2011), p. 17.

Reuters News Staff, "The World's Largest Investors, with $22.5 Call for Climate Change Action," November 20, 2012.

Rosane, Olivia, "Electric Vehicles Sales More than Double in 2017" (Eco Watch).

Rohr, Richard, "Immortal Diamond: Search for Our True Selves" (London, Society for Promotion of Christian Knowledge, 2015).

Sachs, Jeffery, Sustainable Development Solution Network, 2018 SDG Index and Dashboards, A Global Initiative for the United Nations.

Sheed, Frank, *Theology and Sanity* (San Francisco, Ignatius Press, 1946, 1948, 1993), p. 44.

Smith, Adam, "2017 U.S. Billion-Dollar Weather and Climate Disasters: A Historic Year in Context" (*Climate Watch*, January 8, 2018).

United Nations, International Panel on Climate Change, OECD/IEA, 2018.

United Nations, "Islamic Declaration on Climate Change" (August 15, 2015).

Washington Post, "Muslim Leaders Support Islamic Declaration on Climate Change" (August 18, 2015).

Wikipedia, Mondragon Sales.

About the Author

Duane Errol Fleming worked his way through college as an architectural draftsman and earned a Bachelor of Arts degree from Xavier University with an award for excelling in the study of philosophy. He earned a Master's degree in Community Planning from the University of Cincinnati with a minor in economics.

Fleming worked as a Senior City Planner for the cities of Dayton, Ohio and West Palm Beach. He has co-drafted a bill with Representative Robert Wexler, to enable young people to be able to buy a home early in life with a large down payment. The bill, Restore the American Dream Act, HR 3557 is being sponsored by Representative Ted Deutch, who will try to advance the bill as soon as it is practical. This bill features the Home Ownership Plan which will create millions of sustainable jobs and will add billions of dollars to the U.S. Treasury. The Home Ownership Plan was one of 21 finalists out of 22,000 submissions to the national contest, "Since Sliced Bread". However, because of crushing student debt, many young people cannot take on the debt of a mortgage at this time. He has had two articles on the Home Ownership Plan published in the Journal of Housing, and articles in The Christian Science Monitor, The Palm Beach Post, and The Dayton Daily News. Fleming has written one non-fiction book, Building a New America with Christ's Values, published by Westbow Press, in 2014.

Fleming founded and directs the Livelihood Systems Institute (LSI), with the mission to advance job creation and the development of affordable workforce housing and housing for the homeless. For three years, LSI worked with all of the major cities of Ohio to advance funding for affordable housing. Additional funding was provided by the Cleveland Foundation, the George Gund Foundation, and the Standard Oil Company. Fleming lives in Palm Beach Gardens, Florida and keeps a watchful eye on sea level rise and beautiful ocean sunrises.

Printed in the United States
By Bookmasters